Suck Up the
Butter

MW00426359

Copyright © 2002 Donald O Steiger
All rights reserved.

ISBN 1-58898-473-7

Suck Up The Purple Buttermilk

To Mainthe
tdh for for comin
to the week shut
Keep Sacking up the
Purple Buttermilk Your
God Bless Donnie Steeg :)

Donald O Steiger

greatunpublished.com
Title No. 473
2002

Suck Up The Purple Buttermilk

"Don has been where most people could not imagine, and this book is his honest and daunting account of abuse, addiction and recovery."

Table of Contents

"Be pleased O Lord, to <u>deliver</u> me:
O Lord, make haste to <u>help</u> me."

-Psalm 40:13

Author's Acknowledgements

For their valued assistance in completing this project, I wish to thank the following people: John Lynch, for his overall professional input, idea for the title and belief in the purpose of this story. Jim Puz, for his patience and dedication in being responsible for grammar, punctuation, syntax and manuscript format. Amy Puz, for the creation and design of the cover. Carole Womble, Director of the Global Relationship Center in Naples, Florida, for her suggestion to include samples of how I write and spell words in my own unique way. Claire Cousineau, Director of Publishing for Chandler House Press in Worcester, Massachusetts, for her beneficial critique and comments regarding further elaboration in specific areas. My cousin, Rebecca Trelfa (and her husband Jon), for her diligent and skilled work in formatting the manuscript for the e-book and hard copy publication. And finally, to the Photo Lab Technician, Scott Wheeler, and Photographer, Lucinda Young of Express Photo and Portrait Studio in Worcester, Massachusetts for the book's well-done photo reproductions and back cover picture of the writer.

I also want to especially thank my dear family and friends for their continuous support throughout the writing of this straightforward book: my father, Donald E. Steiger; my son, Jesse Otis Steiger and daughter, Amy Lyn Steiger. My Aunt Pat, and her husband, Wally Dash. My Uncle, Dick Becker, the first man to ever seriously talk to me about quitting smoking...and I did! Bill Erickson (and wife Andrea), who demonstrated the importance of steadfast friendship and the value of a dollar! Kevin Huard, a sensational mentor and long-time special friend! Steve Pappas, for his many hours of listening to me voice my concerns with much appreciated tolerance! Steve Connolly, former Worcester resident, now living in Las Vegas as a successful Elvis Impersonator in keeping...the 'Spirit of the King' alive! I planted the seed (idea) for his E-career and it's still always growing...in my great personal friend for many years! All my running buddies at the YMCA! Mary Bean, formally of Spectrum House, who went to bat for me when all the cards read zero, literally saving my neck and my life! Kenneth F. Candito, my probation officer back in the 80's, who successfully utilized a 'tough love' approach with me before the term was ever popular and is currently the Clerk-Magistrate for the Dudley District Court. Pastor Chip Littizzio, his wife Carmen, and Arty Fitzwater of 'His Ministry' outreach.

Forward

by

John Lynch, B.A., Master in Fine Arts

Worcester, Massachusetts native now living and working in Los Angeles, California. He is currently employed by the 'hit series' That 70's Show and involved in several independent film projects

Suck Up the Purple Buttermilk is a story of survival because Don Steiger is alive and well today only by the grace of God. He lived through a childhood of alienation and pain, of confusion and turmoil. From witnessing first-hand the atrocities of the infamous Watt's riots of 1963, to being severely beaten and abused by babysitters and family alike, Don has lived a life that NEEDS to be told. A promiscuous mother that drank, an unstable father who was always on the move, Donnie desperately needed someone to reach out to, someone with whom to share his pain. Sadly, there was no one there.

Don started drinking at an early age and later became addicted to drugs as a teenager and the hellish journey of heroin addiction plagued him for over twenty years. It was only when he lost his closest and dearest friend to an overdose that Don opened his heart to a deeper level of personal faith.

Thank God he did. For now he can share his unbelievable courage through three decades of life on the edge, in the hope of helping other children who see no way out, and other addicts who need someone with whom they can relate.

This is a first person account of a life that changed with

every turn. It is a journey into a man's soul. Donnie shares his most intimate details, and his most horrid memories. Beginning with his childhood, then proceeding through his battle with heroin, and finally his recovery and message of hope. This message is an affirmation of faith, love and triumph over addiction and despair. It displays all the tough, gritty atmospheres of Don's world in realistic, mesmerizing detail. Don has been where most people could not imagine, and this book is his honest, daunting account of abuse, addiction and recovery.

Finally, I would like to make a few closing remarks: When Donnie informed me of his intention to write his memoir, the old adage that everyone thinks their life is a book, initially rang in my head. In any case, I knew nothing of Don's life other than that his father had been friends with one of my favorite actors, Rod Steiger. Therefore, with curiosity, I listened intently to some of the experiences he related to me and I was amazed from the start at this man's life. In turn, I began sharing part of my personal life with him, a victim myself, of extreme identification. I hope that everyone who reads Don's story can take some small piece out of it to better his or her own lives...I know I have.

Introduction

My name is Don and this is a personal story of survival. I am a part Cherokee Indian in my early fifties who lives in Worcester, Massachusetts. Sixteen years ago I could not read or write, today I can. I was once addicted to heroin and alcohol, now I live a normal (whatever that is) drug and alcohol free life.

If you carry away one message, one truth, my wish is that those who feel inadequate, those who need to start every day of their lives with a drug or drink, will discover that there is hope. There is a way UP and OUT of the MADNESS!

Life is short; enjoy the journey while it remains. Don't miss your life by trying to block it out. Do not spend any time worrying about not knowing how to do something, because worry with never make you learn anything, and it sure won't bring anything back. Accepting the journey is the key to a happy life—by asking God for the strength to carry this out—one day at a time.

My advice to the reader: Embrace each day. I am on my journey and you are on yours.

My parents and I (two months old), November 24, 1950.

Dedicated to my mother who has been my greatest teacher, teaching me forgiveness, love, faith, and has given me the greatest gift of all...LIFE!

To Mom Always,

Your Loving Son Donnie

Chapter 1

The Journey Begins

'Time to hit the ground running,
Time to catch the train.
The only time you're satisfied
Is when chaos feeds your brain.'

My name is Don Steiger and I came into this world on September 23, 1950 at 3:20 in the morning. If I knew what was waiting for me, I probably would have tried to stay inside a little longer. The town I was thrown into was called Culver City, California. Don't ask me what I thought of Culver City because I never had a chance to live there. Right after I was born my father bought a house in Hawthorne, a suburb of Los Angeles, home of the Beach Boys and Jan and Dean. Before I even knew what hit me I was on the move. Moving would become as constant as going to the bathroom in my life and I never got used to it.

My mother, a sexy, flamboyant woman named Sue Holeman and my father, the smooth talking ladies man Don 'E." Steiger, were both born somewhere in Tennessee. I never asked where specifically because I don't care. My father was in the Navy during World War II. After the Hiroshima bomb was dropped, my father came home and looked to California to start his "civilian" life. The first thing he did was marry my mother. The two of them started fulfilling the ever-popular American dream of buying a home and raising a family. I was the beginning of their dream. My brother, Eddie, was born eleven months after me, my sister Anita Sue, whom we call Sue, was born one year after him, completing the picture perfect post-nuclear family. But, as we all know, things on the outside are seldom the same on the inside.

The house in Hawthorne was beautiful enough, with a big sunny yard that bordered the Pacific Ocean. In my early years, when I was around five, I remember playing with Eddie and Sue for hours in the California sunlight. Those afternoons of Eddie and I wearing our newly bought Lone Ranger cowboy hats while playing on the swing-set, or sitting on the front porch steps with our dungarees rolled up at the bottom and sporting our duck cuts were happy ones. I really cannot remember any early childhood traumas, I guess the Good Lord was saving them for when I got older.

The only downer I remember early on was that when my brother was six and my sister was four, they were still wetting the bed. My parents, clueless and frustrated, made them wear diapers. Eddie and Sue were embarrassed and humiliated by this. I would tell them not to worry about it, although in a strange sort of way, I felt guilty that I was more 'normal' than they were. This was something I hated seeing them experience, but I felt too powerless over the situation. Even then, I remember wanting to take their problems on as my own. Things in the house were otherwise generally calm. My father had a good job making airplane parts and my mother stayed home most of the time and did her 'motherly' chores. I did not notice a lot of drinking or fighting in the household during my early years. But, as it was with most things in my youth, things changed quickly!

Somewhere around my seventh birthday, the fights started. My father would come home from work and yell at my mother, who had been drinking all day. When my mother was drinking, she would usually be gone all day, coming home late and drunk. Being the oldest at seven, I watched Eddie and Sue all day long and some evenings.

The first thing I noticed on how this was affecting us

was that there was never enough food in the house. Eddie and Sue would constantly ask me, not my parents because of their tempers, for something to eat. Again, I felt responsible to provide, so I decided to go into business at the ripe old age of seven. I knew if I didn't do something, nothing would change. I ventured out, going door-to-door, selling little wooden decorations called 'mothers little helpers' that I was making in our garage. The nickname was later used for the drug, Valium, believed to calm a mother down from her daily stresses. Although I was never a mother, I would take enough mothers-little-helpers in my day to make a hundred mothers never experience stress again! These little wooden shelves went inside the cabinet under the sink. They held cleaning supplies and other kitchen materials. Although my father never received any credit for the invention, mothers-little-helpers are very common nowadays. But fortunately for me, not many people had heard of them back then.

I really wanted to do something to save our family, which was in deep jeopardy, and to keep us fed in the house. My father was working, but between the bills and my mother spending all kinds of cash, we were in tough shape. I was sick and tired of going to bed hungry. There were nights when I would lie in my bed and fantasize about hamburgers and ice cream, tears running down my cheeks. I became obsessed with making these things in the garage to sell. It was in the dark oil-smelling garage, all by myself, that I would spend all my free time. Eddie and Sue were beginning to break by all the problems going on — crying endlessly and panicking. They wanted to know why our parents were fighting and were never home. I'd do my best to keep them calm, believing I had to try to fix the problem. One thing in my favor was that most of our neighbors were obliged to buy my product, some out of interest, most out of pity for the skinny seven-year old kid lugging mothers-little-helpers down the street.

On a brighter note, there were some genuine Hollywood stars that routinely visited our home. Rod Steiger, Marlon Brando's brother in 'On the Waterfront' was my father's friend.

He used to come over for dinner while on break from filming. Sometimes he would bring over such Hollywood new-comers as Steve McQueen, James Garner, Charles Bronson, and Clayton Moore (the Lone Ranger) with whom my father, a magician would later, after his retirement, work in Las Vegas. They would sit at the kitchen table and drink beer. Uncle Rod (as I would call him) and my father served in the Navy Air Corp. He told me WWII was hell, a lot of people died or got wounded really bad. The guys never brought up the horrible word "war" in conversation. Dad mentioned a couple of men he served with; one was a gifted baseball player for the New York Yankees named Joe DiMaggio and the other was a gentleman from the Boston Red Sox by the name of Ted Williams. My heart goes out to all the veterans who put their lives on the line as well as to all the heroes who put the game of baseball on hold in order to serve their country.

Uncle Rod used the G.I. Bill in 1944 to take acting classes in order to improve his opera singing. He told me he loved acting so much that he continued it as a career, becoming one of the most respected actors in Hollywood.

I remember my father asking James Garner why they brought in another actor to play his brother on Maverick. His answer was that he could not remember his lines and, therefore, needed someone else in the scenes so he could have more time to remember the words. They all howled at this. I was only five, but I remember getting a big kick out of seeing them in my kitchen and later on television. All in all, these Hollywood actors were nice to me, but many of them still seemed a little weird.

Our family also used to frequent the now-famous Knoxberry Farm in Anaheim, a short drive south of L.A., which was owned by a close relative of my father. She started the place by selling pies to people and taking children for rides on a horse. Now it is a multi-million dollar business. Riding the horses was perhaps the most fun I had as a kid. Eddie wasn't crazy about the horses but Sue loved them as much as I did. I do not, however, remember anything about the pies!

My mother and father would drink in Corganville, the place where a lot of Hollywood westerns were filmed. Some days I would go with my mother to the bar, my daily lunch consisting of coca-cola and potato chips. The bar was frequented by extras and stuntmen. I started hanging around a little bit with some of the stuntmen's kids. We would go behind the bar and jump off things in the parking lot. I loved it and really believed this was where I wanted to stay for the rest of my life. I felt a certain sense of community and well-being. I felt Corganville was where I belonged.

When I was seven my parents began going out more, both together and alone. They would have strange baby-sitters take care of us, sometimes for days at a time. There were a couple of rough women who used to come over, drunk as skunks, and decide we were dirty children who needed a good cleaning. They would make the three of us strip naked in our backyard and then turn the cold water of the garden hose on us, the neighbors watching, some laughing and some shaking their heads in dismay. Eddie and Sue's screams will always stay with me. As much as I have learned that I can't be truly free until I forgive those who have wronged me, still I have a difficult time forgiving everyone, especially these sadistic baby-sitters.

When they got tired of cleaning the outside of us, they made us eat soap and swallow it, saying it would clean our souls. Sometimes I vomited up soap for hours. Once, after they locked us in the bedroom, I thought Eddie was dying because he violently gagged on the floor next to me! One time, after my mom unexpectedly dropped me off at their house, in resentment, they fed me 'meal' worms with my cereal. Afterwards, I could never eat cereal for many years. Experiences like this would make me feel unloved and unwanted; of being in the way and taking up space that someone else deserved. I began to feel that I would be better off dead. I was afraid if I complained to my parents these women would do something even worse to us. So we kept quiet, something no child who is being abused should ever have to do. But a man does not become a man right away. He is first a child!

All I could do was try to protect Eddie and Sue. I became their guardian at the age of ten. One day I found Sue crying on the front steps. She told me no one would show her how to tie her shoes. So I took the time to gently teach her what I had just recently learned myself. The three of us stuck together like glue. We had to, for we had no idea what was going to happen next.

We eventually lost the house because my father got laid off, my mother up and left us and they were later divorced. My father had custody (my mother never asked for it) and we had to move. My father brought us to live in a series of small, dingy apartments, a far cry from the beautiful home in Hawthorne.

SEAMAN   2nd Class

Donald E. Steiger
U.S. NAVY AIR CORP.
Lake City FLORIDA
(Airplane Mechanic)
2/24/44 through 3/2/46

My father in the Navy during World War II in 1944.

Navy buddies, left to right: Shorty Hawck, Floyd Sands, and my father, Don E. Steiger.

My mother in Hawthorne, California, 1949.

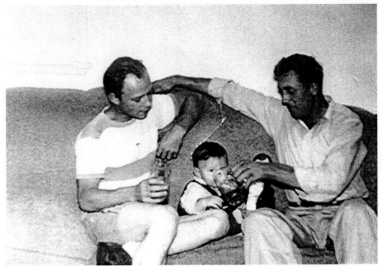

My 'first' drink, at least recorded on photo, left to right: Dad, Me (18 months) and family friend.

Autographed picture of actor, James Garner, to my father Don, with whom he still keeps in touch.

Photograph of well-known screen actor, Rod Steiger, which he sent to my father, Don. The two have resumed contact in recent years.

Steve McQueen in the film 'The Great Escape'.

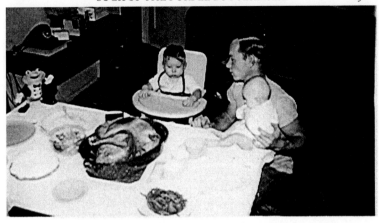

Thanksgiving 1952: myself (age two) and my father, holding my brother Eddie.

Left to right: Eddie and myself, 1954.

Left to right: Eddie and myself, 1957.

Chapter 2

A Boxer Named Jack and A Dog Named Rocket

'Always make the best of things
Sing the chorus and the verse.
Because unless you're breathing your last breath,
Things could always be worse.'

Eddie and I were in school, Sue wasn't. In what is perhaps my biggest argument for the dangers of enabling, my experience with school systems was of being pushed on so quickly that I didn't have time to clap erasers. Even though I could not read or write, they moved me along. First of all, the psychological trauma was set-up from the get go. I was always spending a month in this school and a month in that school, that I felt different from all the other kids. Some teachers would get mad because I was behind the other kids; therefore, a few just passed me on. I was in the fifth grade and still couldn't read or write. The schools in Hawthorne were busy and over-crowded. Being a great con man from an early age, I fiddled and diddled enough to advance each year to the next grade. This had a lot to do with the fact that I was a real good drawer and a not-so-bad storyteller. I remember my fourth grade teacher asking me to bring a piece of paper home to my mother. It was the first time I distinctly recall not just 'feeling' different, but actually realizing I was different. I told the teacher, "I have no mother to bring this home to." When I said it out loud, I understood the sadness in that statement and started to cry!

One day when I came home from school my father was waiting for Eddie and me. Sue was packed and ready to go. It had been decided that we were going to stay with our mother. It seems Dad could no longer afford to support us. My mother was living across town with a thug boxer named Jack and a sheepdog named Rocket. Jack was the kind of boxer that Rocky was at the beginning of the first movie, the one where he fought Spider Rocco. In fact, Jack could easily have been Spider Ricco himself! Jack was an alcoholic, like my mother, but he treated us as well as he possibly could. My idea of being treated well back then was that he never hit us nor was mean to us in any violent or sexual way. His scarred face was pushed in and his lips were permanently swollen. This scared Sue until she got used to his appearance. It seems Jack was in the middle of suing the boxing commission for $100,000.00 for getting hurt in the ring or something like that. He never came clean with the whole story.

I certainly felt out of place living there. We were new in school, once again, I felt different and alone. The teachers would send me to the 'dunce' room and say I was learning impaired and basically labeled me 'retarded'. No one looked at my home life. No one had time! My mother was drinking every day now, with Jack as her constant drinking partner. One night I had to write my name on the top of my homework assignment. I asked Jack and my mom how to spell my name. I was ten years old and hadn't learned yet. My mother was screaming over my shoulder how much of a moron and a loser I was. Jack was as drunk as my mother and he joined in the name-calling. I figured as long as they were yelling at me, instead of Eddie or Sue, that it would be all right, but I still needed to get my name on the top of that paper! Finally Jack grudgingly showed me, swearing and shaking his head at me.

Jack's sheepdog was one of my closest childhood companions. One day I was riding my bike with Rocket faithfully by my side. I watched in horror when I saw him run into the street and bounce off a car bumper! For a few minutes I just sat there on my bike in shock. I didn't know exactly what was going on, but when I cut through the crowd that had gathered, I saw Rocket lying on the pavement bleeding. A policeman came out of nowhere and stooped down to check on my dog. In one quick move, he pulled out his pistol and shot Rocket in the head. It was explained to me later that the policeman had put Rocket out of his misery. I couldn't believe that was necessary. This was the first time I had ever seen that kind of violence and it would not be the last.

Around Christmas that year, Jack got his boxing settlement. A lump sum of cash is an alcoholic's dream, so Jack and Ma excitedly dropped us kids off at their friend's house and went out for a night on the town. Two or three days later we couldn't figure out why they hadn't come to pick us up. Eddie thought they took all the money and ran away. After a week went by, Sue kept asking if our parents were ever coming back. I had no answer. I only kept telling them everything would be fine. Finally, the strangers with whom we were staying told us that Jack and my mother had been in a car accident the same night they dropped us off. The car had flipped over several times. My mother was thrown from the car and it had landed on her. Jack had broken his back but was expected to live. Mother wasn't, which was why they finally told us what was going on.

It was Christmas Eve when we found out the news. My mother had a blood clot in her head and was in critical condition. They eventually let us see her in the hospital but she was in a coma and could not respond. Looking at her shaved head and tubes running up her nose, I felt angry. It was supposed to be a great Christmas that year. Jack and my mother had some money and she promised us tons of presents. It was watching my mother live this kind of life that angered me more than anything else.

Christmas morning we watched my mother's friend's kids open up their gifts as we lay on blankets on the floor. They did give us a small present but I was too angry and hurt to appreciate it. Eddie and Sue looked to me for answers—answers I could not give! We stayed with this family for two months. They weren't bad people but we always felt we were intruding.

We were then placed in a foster home for a year. It was here that I got caught playing with fire. I was angry and wanted to go to my own house. The grandfather of the house, this old burly man with only two fingers on his left hand, kicked my butt for playing with matches. After that, I never played with matches again until I was seventeen. The argument that hitting a child does not work did not apply to this incident.

The bus to and from school drove right past my mother's house where the totaled car sat on the front yard. Every day I saw that smashed-up car and every day it hurt! Jack got out of the hospital sporting a full body cast. We went back to stay with Jack for a little while, but obviously he was not in a parenting position; in fact, the only position he was in was straight on his back! It was decided we should go back with our father and I was psyched!

During this period we were not attending school. Again, no one bothered to find us and make us go. When my mother was released from the hospital she got rid of Jack (and his body cast) and shacked up with a guy named Melvin, whom she apparently met at the hospital. When she settled into Melvin's house, my father took us back to live with her. I asked my father why we couldn't just stay with him. He told me he didn't have enough money to support himself never mind anyone else.

The two things I remember about Melvin were that he had a decent house in Riverbank and had epileptic seizures all the time. This scared Eddie and Sue, but they still preferred to stay with our mother instead of Dad. My mother would go out drinking and leave us home with Melvin. He would have a violent seizure on the kitchen floor then not know where he was for six hours, wandering around in a daze. Other times, Melvin would go out and my mother would have other men over, fooling around with them right in front of me. I would still nurture her back to health whenever her enlarged liver acted up or her head ached.

Sometimes my mother would break out in a fit of rage and beat me. She would choose me for a variety of reasons; I was the oldest and I looked like my father. The object of her beatings was to make me cry. When I didn't, she would beat me harder. I remember Eddie and Sue watching my mother beating me with a belt, with blood running down my ears. They were screaming "Cry Donnie! Cry Donnie!" I always waited until I wore my mother out and returned to my room before I bawled. Needless to say, I wanted to go back with my father, but Eddie and Sue were willing to stick it out with my mother and Melvin. I couldn't understand why!

We were with Melvin and my mother the day my sister almost drowned. Behind Melvin's house were a series of canals, which every now and then filled up with water. There were cement bridges that had about a half-inch space at the top through which debris could float. While playing on the bridge during a family picnic, Sue fell into the canal. Eddie and Melvin had no idea how to swim. My mother, who couldn't swim a lick either, yelled at the top of her lungs, "Donnie! Donnie! What are we going to do Donnie?"

Again, at age twelve, I was responsible for taking care of everything. She did not yell for Mel, it was my job. So I jumped into the canal not caring if I lived or died because I was only concerned for Sue! I remember seeing on television how some New York cop had grabbed a guy wanting to commit suicide by jumping off the Brooklyn Bridge. In doing so, he almost sacrificed his own life. When asked why he would jeopardize his own existence for that of a stranger, he replied, saying, in so many words, there was no thought process involved, only an instinct that tells you what needs to be done. Since Sue was not a stranger to me, I jumped into the canal thinking only of saving her at any cost! I found her totally submerged under the water panicking. I swam under her and put my shoulders under her feet and, with all my strength, pushed her towards the shore. She flew to the side of the canal and Melvin grabbed her. She lay on the shore, puking water and gasping for air. That was the day I learned how to swim, a little on the job training.

Shortly after this incident my father came to visit. I missed him and wanted to go back to living with him. I was sick of hunting my mother down at her bars and begging five dollars off her for food. I was definitely sick of Melvin and his attacks.

Sometimes she and Melvin would leave us alone for weeks at a time. One day a gas stove blew across the room as we tried to cook english muffins. We had no idea about pilot lights or anything like that. If I couldn't find my mother, we stole bread and bologna from the market. Eddie was a better thief than Sue or myself, but we all knew how to do what we needed to do to survive.

When my father came to visit I begged him to take us back and he always said no. I pretended to accept his answer, yet, deep down, I knew that he wasn't leaving without me. When no one was looking I hid under the floorboards in the back of his car. After my father drove on the highway for about an hour I peeped my head up. Maybe I wasn't as good a thief as Eddie, but I was learning street smarts. I knew Eddie and Sue would be all right because, for some ungodly reason, they wanted to stay with Ma. My father couldn't believe he had a stowaway with him on this way to Los Angeles. If I had known what L.A. would be like, I probably would have stayed with Mom.

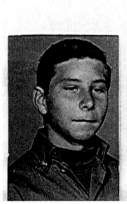

School pictures left to right: myself (12), Susie (9) and Eddie (11).

Chapter 3

Welcome to the Jungle

'No time to waste, no time to run
Peace of mind, I never had none.
The future's uncertain, hand me that gun.
Who am I? My father's son.'

I temporarily got my wish to live with my father. Los Angeles was a world that I had never before experienced. There was violence and weirdoes everywhere. We were sleeping in the body shop where my father was working, doubling as security guards in the evenings. It was one long room with a single window looking out onto Main Street with paper-thin walls. There was a bar across the alley to which my father would bring me sometimes, introducing me to glasses of beer and pinball machines at the age of twelve.

In the room, my father slept on one side of the cot and I slept on the other. I slept with a loaded 22 rifle next to me, my father slept with his pistol. One night a piece of rotting plaster from the ceiling fell on my father. He woke up firing, bullets flying around the room. When we realized what had happened, we shared a nervous laugh. Sometimes Dad would leave me there alone all weekend and I would lie there at night with the gun pointed toward the door, ready to shoot at the first intruder. I don't know what you were doing at twelve, but I'm pretty sure it wasn't this!

Another evening while my father was frequenting the bar

across the alley, someone did try to break in. I heard a noise at the end of the room, a rattling coming from the window. When I adjusted my eyes to the darkness, I realized that someone was actually halfway through the window. Scared, I screamed at the top of my lungs and freaked out! In one quick movement, I raised my rifle and began firing at the window. To this day, I have no idea if I killed someone that night, since the person who tried to break in fled the scene.

Later in my life I would make the decision never to touch a gun again. My father would even buy me a shotgun and ask me to go hunting, but I refused to ever have anything to do with guns. I would come to see nothing but disaster as a result of gunplay, including a friend at school who shot and killed another friend over a five-dollar card game. Although I understand the need for protection that a gun can provide, my personal belief is that there are always other means to keep yourself safe.

One night my father came home bloodied and beaten. He had been stabbed in the hand and a bottle opener keyed his face. We had no bandages or first aid equipment, so I wrapped the wounds in socks. I missed Eddie and Sue, but knew in my heart this was no place for them.

My father told me to get back to school, for it had been over a year since being in one. He enrolled me in Gompers Junior High. It was a high school and junior high rolled into one. There were only three non-black kids in the school and I was one of them. Besides me, there was a white woman and a Mexican woman. I once told some of my black friends that I know what it's like to be a minority. If I already had a sense of uniqueness, you can imagine what if felt like now.

There were constant threats of violence towards me. I hired a bodyguard. A big black football player named Lenk, short for Lecan, to walk me around school. Things were tough, and I was involved in a lot of fights. I would go up the stairs at school with my books in hand, only to be shoved back down by a bunch of angry punks at the top. I would silently pick up my books and make another attempt, only to have it done over and over again. Finally, they would tire and move on, because they were worn down from my lack of response. In class girls would look at me as though I were an alien and the boys would spit on me and call me every name in the book. This didn't bother me as much as you might think—I was quite numb already.

The administration wasn't any better. I was 'swatted' frequently in school. When anyone was late, the principal would take him or her down to his office and hit him or her with a heavy paddle in the behind. This was called 'swatting'. Occasionally, they would ask me to read and write something, which I was unable to do. They would send me to special classes in order to shuffle me through the system. I was already a year behind with a fourth grade reading level.

There was no segregation in the United States and President Kennedy wanted to send Watts students to better schools. This provided hope to a lot of inner-city kids, but before this went any further, Kennedy was shot. I was sitting in a classroom when the announcement came over the speaker that Kennedy had been shot in the head. I was rushed out of school and sent home where my father was waiting. No one knew what repercussions this would have on American society.

For the next two years, I lived from day to day, minute to minute. Finally, Eddie and Sue came to live with us. It was great to see them again, although I knew this living arrangement was only temporary. It seems my mother was running around with Tommy Claybough, the leader of the California chapter of the Hell's Angels. He was living with my mother for a while in his place, during her fights with Melvin, and I spent some time with him while I was bouncing back and forth. He disciplined us by taking us out in the yard to fight. He even did this with Sue. Tommy was another guy with whom my mother had sex right in front of us; there were many other times too! Eddie and Sue soon got sick of this and Tommy grew sick of them, as well, which is why they came to live with us. My mother eventually became tired of Tommy and went back to live with Melvin.

There was no way the four of us could sleep in the auto body shop for too long. Eddie and Sue, although looking thin and tired, seemed to be all right. Still, we were all together again and what little understanding I had of family, was present in my life again. Unfortunately this was short-lived because soon after Eddie and Sue's arrival, the infamous Watts riots went down in August of 1965—where entire sections of Los Angeles were burned to the ground. A total of 201 buildings were destroyed by fire and 536 other buildings had been damaged or looted. The total cost of the property damage was estimated at $40 million. People were killing one another in the streets. My father read to us that Neita Love, a sixty-seven year old woman driving a car with her husband, got nervous when police tried to stop her at a barricade on Avalon Boulevard. When she panicked and accelerated, she was shot and killed. Our family was escorted out of the neighborhood in a two-machine-gun jeep. From the jeep, I remember seeing two boys from my class walking down the street with a little red wagon filled with newly looted vodka bottles. That was my last childhood memory of Los Angeles.

We headed back to Hawthorne with our father, moving into a hotel across from the high school. I was now fifteen and had the reading and writing ability of someone half my age, but I was learning to hide it better. I became interested in athletics and dreamed of becoming a professional stunt man. I nearly killed myself a few times in my youth, inventing stunts from the back porches and roofs of our apartments.

I liked to workout in the gym at school but didn't like the crowded, smelly locker room. I asked a friend for a way to get on the football team. He told me the roster was already complete but I learned that there were some openings on the cross-country team. I went to the coach and asked to be on the team. He said I could try out if I cut my hair. I told him that if he wanted my hair cut, he would have to do it. So he grabbed the scissors and gave me a haircut. With short hair and a good running ability, I made the team.

To this day I can still hear the coach yelling," Suck up the purple buttermilk! Suck up the purple buttermilk!" This was his macho blurb to get us to not be wimps. Every year they would make him a glass of purple buttermilk using food coloring and he would drink it down. This was the first time in all my experiences at school that I felt a part of something. I became the leading runner on the team.

Also, around this time, I began to experiment more with alcohol. Of course, it was always around the house, so I started testing the waters and enjoyed the warm glow that a couple of shots could bring me. Sometimes I would show up at practice a little buzzed, but no one picked up on it. One time, after a few shots of Old Granddad, I heard the phone ringing in the apartment. I got off the couch and drunkenly fell to the floor, crawling over to the phone in what I thought to be an amusing stupor.

My lack of study ability eventually caught up to me. The school told me I could no longer be on the track team because of my grades. If I raised my grades I could go to the next track meet, otherwise I was out. How could I possibly learn to read or write in the next two weeks? I was angry and hurt. The day of the meet I was sitting in class and raised my hand to go to the bathroom so I could run out and meet the team. I had my gym bag packed and ready to go. I got on the bus and when the coach yelled roll call and came to my name he said, "Wait, Steiger's not here" and crossed my name off the list. I spoke up and said, "Here coach!" He looked at me and shook his head, saying, "You're not here." He then let the bus roll with me on it. During the ride the coach came over and asked me to join the junior varsity team. I couldn't believe it! The coach understood that, in most cases, bad grades at Hawthorne meant a horrific home life, which was definitely a right call in my case. He not only bent the rules for me, he set me up with a tutor so I could join the team. I was in again!

My father called the running a waste of time. He always wanted me to play football. Every week I asked my father to come to a meet. He was working out of our apartment doing phone sales directly across the street from the high school and could see the meets from our window. All he had to do was open his window to see me run by. Every meet I watched the window and every time there was no one in it. Once again, it hurt to know the man I had always fought to live with wouldn't even acknowledge what I was doing.

The school had an awards banquet at the end of the season and the coach told me I was getting a trophy. When my father came home the night of the banquet, he saw me getting all dressed up. He asked me where I was going and I told him. He was shocked that I was actually good at running. He asked me if I wanted him to come but I told him not to bother since I had already begged him repeatedly to attend. The trophy was my was of saying, "screw your football, Dad." He ended up coming anyway and that night was one of the happiest of my youth. My advice for all kids out there who find it hard to fit in, grab onto a sport, any sport, for it will change (and may even save) your life.

My father watched me go to the podium and afterward I could see tears in his eyes. He gave me a big hug, as he whispered in my ear, "I still wished you had played football." I wasn't going to let him spoil my evening, so I let it go and accepted the moment. That night I felt a connection with my father, which I had never before experienced. He apologized and said he was proud of me; we were friends.

It was around this time that girls started looking really good to me. I started getting close to some, but we never really stayed in one place too long. My father would get behind in the rent or into some trouble at a bar and therefore, we would pack up and move to another neighborhood. This did not help my relationships with females at all.

By now, my drinking had started to increase. I was hanging around with a kid named Jimmy who lived a couple of apartments down from me. His sister would buy us bottles of brandy. I had never tried it before, but loved it from the get go. Jimmy's parents were never home, which gave us a safe place to drink. We also went to the beach, where we would skateboard and surf. Eddie and Sue came with us sometimes and we had a blast soaking up the California rays. Eddie made friends quickly but I didn't, so I sometimes would intrude on his friendships. This caused a few arguments, but Eddie and I never really had any major fights.

One Christmas in Hawthorne stands out in particular. Eddie and I were constantly playing tricks with each other. I took a heavy piece of steel from the backyard and wrapped it in Christmas paper. Eddie would pick it up every day and wonder what it was. I told him it was something that he was going to love. When he opened it on Christmas morning he chased me around the room because he was so angry! Our father gave Eddie drumsticks and me a guitar. It seemed Dad wanted us to get into the music scene. I learned a few chords, but what I really loved to do was tap on the back of it as if it were a drum. Eddie couldn't keep a beat to save his life, but I could. I had no interest in the guitar but I kept it anyway. My first set of drums was composed of pots and pans, with an old cooler as a base drum. I played along with this new band known as the Rolling Stones, as well as the Beach Boys and Jan and Dean. The beach anthem "Wipeout" was my favorite tune to play on my handmade drum set!

I was fifteen now and didn't like the way I looked. I was constantly trying to change my outside appearance through working out and running. I had deep feelings of inferiority and didn't like myself. I believe everyone goes through a stage when they can't stand their looks, but mine seemed stronger than it did for most of the teens I knew.

It was around this time that my mother came looking for us. Melvin had apparently died in the bathtub after a seizure and she instantly hooked up with another guy. My father told me that my mother found us and wanted to see us. I had no desire to see her. I remember her smell. When my mother came into the room to see me, I smelled the same perfume I used to smell when she was getting ready to go out. She would sit in front of the mirror for twenty minutes and spray herself with perfume and hair spray. To this day, hair spray triggers thoughts of my mother. Eddie and Sue were not thrilled to see her this time either. When we told her we wanted to stay with Dad, she got angry and called us 'ungrateful brats', storming out of the house!

I was getting frustrated that I couldn't read or write, so

I stayed up late in the evenings trying to read comic books. No sooner after setting up a tutor appointment at school, we moved again from Hawthorne to Izeusas near the San Bernadino Mountains. I believe my father wanted to stay one step ahead of my mother, and rightly so! There was no telling what she was going to do next. It was constantly eighty-five degrees and always sunny. My father rented a house and got a new job. I had my own room! I had my own choice of wallpaper, so I used Playboy centerfolds, a sixteen year olds' dream!

I started drinking even more at this time after I ran into my friend Tommy with whom I used to work out. He drank his father's stash and I joined him. Again, I felt like life was all right after a couple of beers, it really seemed harmless. In the garage I made myself another drum set. I spent hours listening to The Stones and beach stuff. One day I was in the living room playing my favorite radio station when my father came in screaming. He picked up my stereo and ripped it out of the wall. In one quick motion he smashed it into a thousand pieces on the floor. I turned around and hit him square in the face. I had never stood up to anyone before. He crashed against the wall and slowly slid down the wall. I yelled at him, telling him if he ever touched anything of mine again I would kill him. When he started to come to, he told me I was going to reform school. Eddie and Sue came into the room and began crying. Sue told me," You're in trouble now Donnie." All I said was things couldn't get any worse than this. I was scared but would not back down from him. He never made the call, but decided he'd better get his kids out of this California environment.

Chapter 4

Going East

'Going to the country,
We have to anyway.
Packing our belongings,
This time we're going to stay.'

Everyone needs help once in a while. Asking for assistance does not mean you are a bad person or that you are losing your independence. It is a healthy person that can accept and be grateful for help. God loves you exactly the way you are.

I guess my father thought it was the west coast's fault that I had knocked him out. My father's mother lived in Greenfield Massachusetts so he decided to take us there to live. There was plenty of trouble in Izeusas, California that may have prompted our cross-country move because the house we were staying in was a disaster area and Dad was once again behind on the rent. We packed up the old station wagon and left everything else there. My father put Sue on a plane and told her we would meet her at Grandma's. I remember pulling out of Izeusas and going to L.A., watching that black smog smother the city. Before we left, my father gave me a bravado example of self-will. "See this cigarette," he snickered. "This is the last one you will ever see me smoke." He squashed the filter with his cowboy boots and that was the last time I saw my father smoke.

The '62 Plymouth station wagon, which my father had

painted blue with white trim around the windows, looked like a house. Every couple of days the head gasket would go and we had to park somewhere so my father could fix it. We drove and drove and drove! I remember that the Mojave Desert was the most beautiful thing I ever saw as a child. I heard somebody once say that you can always find God in the desert and I know what he meant.

Roaring down the infamous highway 61, I was astounded to see black people still in the fields picking cotton. I also saw a brother and sister having sex with a group of people watching them. I just couldn't understand any of this. The head gasket in the Plymouth blew again and we pitched a tent in a parking lot. Reminiscent of living in the body shop in Los Angeles, my father and I slept with guns. That night I woke up hearing whizzing noises and thought a bug had made his way into the tent. The whizzing sounds were bullets. My father was whispering, "We're being shot at! Donnie shoot back!," while he crawled over to Eddie and me. I grabbed the gun and started to fire back, and like the time in the body shop, I had no idea if I killed someone. I can only pray that I didn't!

We visited some of my father's family in Tennessee. I met my uncle, a big, filthy man who walked with a major limp. When I asked him why he limped, he brought me into the garage and showed me a huge sickle. Then he smiled and pointed to 'the bad boy' that took a couple of inches off his leg. This is all I remember about this visit.

After two days, the car continued on towards Massachusetts. One night my father fell asleep at the wheel after driving for two days straight. He mumbled something like "take the wheel Eddie" and passed out. Sitting in the middle and half asleep, in horror, I saw a tree coming our way. I grabbed the steering wheel and quickly turned it, causing the car to fish tail, barely avoiding an accident, but not before spinning around several times! Between spending seven straight days with a guy who just quit smoking, along with the fact that none of us had showered for days, the trip was fast becoming a little annoying.

We came into Massachusetts through the Mohawk Trail.

It was the beginning of summer, but the air was cool with a little mist. My father was telling us stories about snow and great winters, trying to make us feel better about the move, but I was not going to forgive him that easily. I turned sixteen while we were driving cross-country and I was already tired from life on the road.

Finally, the mallard blue Plymouth pulled into Aunt Pat and Uncle Bud's driveway on Lampblack Road. Sue was already there and anxiously awaited our arrival with the rest of the family. I can honestly say that while living with my Aunt Pat, I experienced unconditional love for the first time. She made us feel like her home was ours, a feeling I never before experienced. It was a huge house; Sue, Eddie and I had a big room to share.

My father went to town and got a job right away. Bud was a hard knocks kind of guy. My cousin said that the army had made him that way. He and my father became drinking buddies, sucking down 'Black Labels' by the dozens. This, of course, meant that I became one too. I used to hear my father saying to Bud, " I can't believe we drank all that beer!" They didn't, I helped.

When school was mentioned, my stomach started to growl. Once again, I had to stand before the class and be introduced as the new student, hoping to be treated as one of the bunch. I was dreading the day it would be discovered that I couldn't read or write. When I enrolled in Greenfield High School, I was like a tiger having come out of the jungle, becoming more and more angry as time passed. The only thing I could think of was how to get back to California. I was mad at my father and mad at my mother. I was just plain mad. The one good thing that happened: I made a friend right away, a Robert Plant look-alike by the name of Steve Quinlavan. I could relate to Steve because he, like myself, suffered abuse by a parent. His father, when drunk, would beat him, often times leaving cuts and bruises on his body.

I made some makeshift drums and practiced every night. My Aunt Pat would watch me practice, telling me over and over how good I played. Pat was a talented singer herself. She used to sing Connie Francis songs in the living room. We had what we called 'Steiger Talent Night' on Saturday nights. Her daughter, Janice, used to act out skits, my father did his magic tricks, calling himself 'Steiger the Magician'. Aunt Pat would sing with me playing the drums. My cousins were Sandy, Janice, Robin, and the youngest was Steven. We all got along very well and I thank them to this day for all their acceptance and unconditional love. It was a real hoot playing with all of them and watching them perform various skits on talent night. Eddie was playing the guitar and even Sue picked it up for a while. There was one thing you could always say about my youth, it was never dull.

In school though, I was becoming a tyrant. I was enrolled as a freshman and doing my best not to let anybody know how stupid I was. The seniors used to come into our shop class before they would go out to learn carpentry. During this time they bullied the younger kids around. One morning a senior was giving a freshman a hard time. He kept telling the shy kid, "C'mon, you chicken, hit me right here!" pointing at his chin. I walked over and stood between them. The senior was much bigger than me, but I looked him straight in the eye and stupidly said, "I'll tell you what—I'll hit ya." doing my best John Wayne. He looked at me and snickered, "Okay, mighty mouth, hit me right here." I pretended to walk away and then turned and nailed him good! He stumbled against the wall, half-unconscious, and lunged at me. The shop teacher, Mr. Vassil, whom we called Vaseline, came roaring out of the office, his one eyebrow rose as high as it could go, but for some unknown reason, he just stood there letting the fight continue as if it were something out of a western movie. We flew around the room trading blows and suddenly he hit me real hard in the face causing me to stumble just before he put both hands together and clocked me in the head. I saw red, maybe some of my own blood, and then jumped on him. After that Mr. Vassil broke up the fight. We had to go down to the office and have our picture taken with our arm around each other in a friendly manner. They were not used to violence in Greenfield and, therefore, did not know what to do about it. I'll never forget my face looking like a billboard for beaten children!

Around this time, I saw my first snow. It was the strangest thing I had ever experienced. Eddie, Sue and I were worn out playing for hours in the ice and snow. I was hanging around Steve Quinlavin most of the time doing more and more drinking and, to me, it was becoming really fun. Eddie and Sue were making friends and going to school; although Sue was doing rather better than Eddie, none of us could read a newspaper or write a paper like most of our peers.

Life went on, motherless on the East Coast. When I turned seventeen, my father got me a job in a tobacco plant for the summer. He was seeing one of Pat's friends and decided to move closer to her. We finally moved out of Pat's home and into a house right down the road. My father was seldom home and I saw this as a perfect opportunity to drink. My job consisted of picking tobacco in the hot sun by tying a gunny sack to my waste and scooting on my backside through the fields picking and stacking the leaves. Working with a bunch of nice Mexicans who could not speak English, they always bought me beer at lunch.

One day I cut my foot badly, but when I informed the straw boss (the boss in the field) he told me to get back to work. When I mentioned that I was too injured to work, he yelled for me to get back in the field and pick tobacco. Bending over to remove my boot, he kicked me in the back. I went into a rage and, after spitting in his face, he said I was fired; but I told him I couldn't be fired because I quit! The tobacco was stuck to my face and arms and the temperature was at least ninety degrees. I stormed down the road on foot and suddenly a big black Cadillac pulled up to me. The window rolled down, the guy asked me, "What's your problem?" All I could say was that the straw boss was an idiot (but using a less flattering term)! With a twenty-mile walk back home, I did it and never looked back again.

On Friday nights there would be a dance at school. I would take with me an empty bottle with a lid and mix different kinds of alcohol, which served as my buzz for the evening. I had bought a set of drums with what little money I had made picking tobacco and belonged to a band called the 'Sundowners'. We played little bars in Greenfield, rocking to such classics as 'Money Money', 'Louie Louie' and some surf songs. During these ventures I was given a lot of free booze and tried marijuana for the first time. But one Friday night we had nothing to drink, so I stole a bottle from the liquor store. Unbeknownst to me, it was cooking sherry, but all I knew was that it was alcohol. Steven didn't drink anymore after his first gulp (I wonder why) so I proceeded to drink the whole bottle. By the time we got to the dance, I could not play drums, period! Somehow though, I felt important, like a real rock star, Keith Moon, for example. Yet I didn't feel so important after being sick for the next thirteen hours.

One night I was playing drums in the attic, when all of a sudden my father came charging at me with a knife. He was inflamed and apparently wanted to slice up my drum set. I looked him in the eye and told him that I would kill him if he touched my set. He saw how serious I was and backed off. This incident reminded me again of Steve's father beating up on him. His mother was one of those quiet types who kept her mouth shut because she, out of fear for her safety, was too afraid to confront her husband. I felt so bad for him whenever I went to his house and saw his face beaten and swollen.

I met another drummer, named Tobey, and would walk about five miles to his house to play drums. He had a very nice mother and a great set of drums. One day after coming home from Tobey's, my father told me we were moving to Worcester, Massachusetts, quite a ways from Greenfield. I let him know I was not moving anywhere. To me, this was the last straw! I had grown comfortable there in the western part of the state, having friends and a band that made me feel 'I belonged'. My father wanted to marry the woman he'd been seeing and since she was moving to Worcester, so were we. I couldn't believe that he was doing this to us again. Not only did I have friends and a band, I now had a new girlfriend, Holly, now it was being ripped away! I don't know what is worse, being loved for a few years or not knowing love at all; either way it hurts!

My father said I had to go. After the move I was so angry, I started being self-destructive by sniffing glue and gasoline, smoking and drinking even more booze. I didn't even want to try anymore or get close to another person again, what was the point? I became emotionally and mentally depressed. My father's girlfriend, Barbara, had three kids --Beanie, Jeanie and Bookie—who lived with us. Since they were younger than the three of us, they required more attention, which put us on the back burner. This made me feel hurt, angry and worse, lonely. All I really wanted was someone to give me a hug and tell me everything is all right. Barbara wasn't mean to us but she just naturally spent more time with her own children. It was difficult to look at her as a mother because she was young looking and, I thought, kind of sexy; definitely not the mother type. My father was drinking heavily again and any attempt at a normal family life was marred by his drunkenness.

'It's a lot easier to OVERDO something
than it is to UNDO it!"

I went to school one day and realized I couldn't go on like this anymore. On the bus ride home with Eddie, I knew this would be my last day in Worcester. I told Barbara the next morning that I was sick, so after she left me home alone, I packed a quick suitcase and headed for Greenfield, fifty miles west. At seventeen and a half, all I cared about was leaving this messed up life of mine. My father was so angry about my running away, he never bothered looking for me.

As I entered the town where I had a true sense of belonging, I lay low, sleeping in Salvation Army bins and various other hide-a-ways. I hated everybody for not coming to look for me with each passing day. Even if they had found me, I probably wouldn't have gone back. This ever-constant anger turned inward created depression. I decided at this point, to slowly kill myself through drugs.

I started hanging around with Arty, a dope smoker, shooting speed intravenously and taking any pill I could get my hands on. Arty and I would take the bus to Boston and cop drugs in the 'combat zone' where Arty knew some people who were more than happy to take our money. Our intention was to bring the drugs back to Greenfield in order to sell them, but, of course, we consumed them immediately upon our return.

I found a part-time job and got a room in downtown Greenfield for eight-dollars a week. Steve eventually left his dysfunctional home and took a room in the same building. I remember watching the news about Woodstock in 1969 on a little black and white television that belonged to Steve. I was totally blown away by what I saw, which confirmed to me that partying was the only way to go! We both began going to Boston every weekend, living on the streets, sleeping in graveyards and Salvation Army clothing boxes. It was the sixties and you could meet various people to party with for weeks at a time.

During this period, I had to get on a bus with other hippies and head to Springfield to see if we were going to Vietnam. The echoes of 'Alice's Restaurant' were ringing in my brain. They called me in a room and an officer asked me if I ever did drugs. I gladly told him I did everything and he could see the marks on my arm from using speed. He looked at me and asked me more stupid questions and then said for me to get back on the bus. I asked him what this meant and he said, "Donald Steiger, what this means is, the United States Army does not require your services. Have a good life." And with that he got up and left the room. This was, so I thought, the best thing that drugs ever did for me. I said nothing on the bus back, because I knew most of the guys were heading overseas.

Back in Greenfield I met a girl by the name of Debby at a party who took me back to her pad. She wanted me to have sex with her and agreed to pay me for it. She and her older sister used to have me cop drugs for them, after which, we would all get stoned. She said I could stay at her pad as long as I slept with her. At seventeen, I lost my virginity to Debby, not knowing anything about love. Sex became like any of the other drugs I was using: a quick way to feel good.

I stayed put in Greenfield for a while, playing music on occasion and, eventually, getting in another band. One night at a band party things got pretty ugly because a couple of band members grabbed a girl and started forcing her down on the floor. I ran over to the guys and pulled them off of her. I told her to leave and she ran away hysterically. I really did not want to hurt other people and would do anything possible to stop needless violence, but this lifestyle could only breed trouble.

On one Friday evening, we were getting drunk up on a hill when I spotted a tobacco field in the distance. I told the guys that I was going to burn it down and they said I wouldn't dare. Not willing to back down, I grabbed a couple of beers and ran down the hill, lit a match and threw it on the screen coverings. They went up in seconds! My friends (accomplices I like to call them) took off. After running back up the hill I passed out. Today I feel it was the hate I carried for that straw boss in the tobacco field that caused me to light the match. My pride of not asking for help festered inside of me until it turned destructive. When I awoke, I was alone and the field was burning down to the ground as I ran back to my room.

A couple of weeks later, after taking two hits of orange wedge acid, I was tripping and hanging out with the guys on the corner. I was getting off seeing various colors coming to life. This was the strangest drug I ever ingested because the acid high I experienced induced a pure hallucinating brainwash! Getting high like this was quickly becoming a regular routine.

Meanwhile, in this condition, I got in a car with my friends to drive around killing time. Out of nowhere, a police car pulled us over and asked if my name was Don Steiger. By now, I wasn't too sure who I was, but was able to mumble something that sounded like 'yes'. They said there were a couple of questions that needed to be answered by me, so they put me in the cruiser and brought me downtown. Tripping inside the police station was one of the weirdest moments I ever had because people's faces were melting and the lights were like rainbows. Pulsating and vibrating, I looked at the faces of the cops through rows of plaid wallpaper streaming to a river of colors onto the wax floor with echoing sounds, managing to just try to understand this was a miracle in itself!

The policemen kept asking me over and over about the tobacco field. Finally, wanting them to stop talking so I could continue my trip, I confessed that I burned down the field. In two weeks I would be eighteen and the day of my birthday I walked into the courtroom. The judge gave me thirty days in the Franklin County Jail. This would be my first conviction but certainly not my last. But one thing would be my last and that is: I would never again experiment with any more hallucinatory drugs (I had stopped counting after a hundred).

Earlier, I had befriended a street wino named Joseph, giving him a few bucks for a drink. When I got settled in jail, I saw Joseph, in from the cold due to some infraction of the law. He showed me the ropes and I kept close to him. I got a job in the laundry room, which was cool, because it made the time pass quicker. I remained sober in jail, even attending AA meetings, but having no clue as to what they were saying. One important thing I did do while there, I started trying to learn how the read and write. I wrote my family a letter with the help of other inmates. My brother Eddie received one and came to visit me. I thanked him for coming but told him not to come anymore; I didn't want him to see me in there like that.

Chapter 5

The Viscous Cycle

'You can have this stupid life,
You can have this town.
The more I try to understand,
The farther I go down.'

When I got out of jail, I moved into a rooming house in Greenfield owned by a woman having the notable name of Isabelle Fairhurst. Her husband had been a big whig (big shot), a political genius who died and left her a lot of property. She invited me to come and live in her barn. Every morning I would go in the house and talk to her. She always had a bottle of whiskey hidden under her pillow. She used to love to listen to us playing music in the barn. It was while living there that my drug use took off big time. Sometimes I was dancing on speed for two or three days straight and other times, I would see images or hear voices, which were not even there, often talking non-stop to no one for hours.

I also began partying with a black dude I met in jail who looked like Jimi Hendrix. One day he took out some droppers, because, in those days, junkies shot drugs using eyedroppers. We would roll up a cut from a dollar bill and put it on the tip of the dropper. We then put a needle on the end of the bill and stuck it in our arm. If you hit a vein you saw a flag, which meant, a red ball of blood in the dropper signifying pay dirt. You slowly squeezed the dropper and let the drugs enter your veins. I did speed using that method and it was like kissing the face of God back then. Jimi took out some heroin and did a dropper full. He left me some in the cooker, the bottle cap where he mixed heroin with water. I did half a dropper and when that puppy hit my brain all my worries and fears left me! Instantly, I realized my new passion—copping heroin. There was also blue morphine and other similar drugs to kill the pain. These turned out to be the 'god' I was searching for all my life.

Artie, another junkie, loved doing smack too. At parties we would line up like kids waiting for a treat and he would hit us with a needle. We called him 'The Doctor'. One day we were walking down the street high as a kite on speed when Artie spotted two guitars inside a car. After we grabbed the axes (guitars) from the back seat and ran around the corner, the police car was waiting there for us, tipped off by an anonymous caller. Jail time number two—another 30 days to serve!

They booked us for larceny, stealing over a hundred dollars worth of stuff. Every time I went to jail my attitude worsened. I realized that this was becoming a pattern or ritual and I hated it. I hung out with a proverbial troublemaker, Eddy Lucier, who spent every winter in jail and every summer outside. He was always in trouble and always got me in trouble.

"Even when you're free, you may still be confined!!"

I remember watching 'The Birdman of Alcatraz', starring Burt Lancaster, in the recreation room one night. Eddy kicked over an ashtray near me and yelled some profanities. The screw (guard) came over to me and told me to get up. They placed me in solitary for two weeks. That night I knew there was no such thing as justice in jail. Every Wednesday and Friday were visiting days, but I never got a visit.

Once again, I had some of the inmates help me with my reading and writing. I also made drumsticks out of duct tape and popsicle sticks and played music with some of the others, mostly kids like me in their late teens and early twenties.

One morning I woke up and doubled over with severe

stomach pain. I thought I was just having withdrawal symptoms. I complained to the screws, but they didn't care a bit; for three days I was in extreme agony, yet no one came to help. I freaked out, throwing everything in my cell out into the corridor. I kept screaming, "I'm dying! Help me!" Still no one responded. I had been puking yellow bile for days.

The pain was so bad that I wanted to die. I put my head in the toilet until I passed out. When I woke up the doctor was pushing on my stomach and each time he did so, I screamed loudly! The doctor told the guards to get me to the hospital immediately, as I heard him say I didn't have much time. Here it was, I thought, the end of the line. As they drove me to the hospital, the nurses kept asking me family information. I told them to get away from me, since I wondered why my family even mattered. I was given Demerol to calm me down and as I looked at the end of my bed, there stood two more doctors and a priest. I knew I was dying!

The doctor asked me to tell him the truth about taking drugs. I told him I had not taken any since I started my sentence six days ago. He told me that my appendix had burst and my body was full of poison. They would do everything in their power to save me. They then proceeded to prep me for surgery. The priest followed behind my stretcher, saying prayers out loud. When I woke up, I was in such unbelievable pain, I could hardly stand it! I had tubes in my nose and IV's everywhere. I also had a guard outside my room, as if I were going anywhere. My mouth was very dry—I needed water badly. Then I sensed that someone was there putting straw in my mouth. It was my Aunt Pat who stood there crying. Unable to talk, I just stared at her, as if trying to say things will be all right.

With her daughter Janice standing behind her, Aunt Pat kept telling me that she loved me and then gave me a wooden cross from Bethlehem, putting it around my neck and kissing me. From that moment on, I started recovering and to this day, still carry that cross with me.

Since I could barely walk, they began giving me intense physical therapy. I remember trying to go for a walk with these little paper slippers, "shooshing" all over the hospital. I can still hear those slippers crunching on the hospital floor. One time I heard my name on the loud speaker to return to my room, so I 'swooshed' back as quickly as I could. The next day they shipped me back to jail. When I saw Arty, I told him what had happened to me. Another inmate came up to me and said I was a sissy. After telling him to shut up, he punched me really hard in the gut. Falling to the floor, Arty helped me back to my cell. WELCOME BACK: with my life threatened, what could I expect, this was jail!

Once I got released from jail, I went back to my room at Isabelle's. My friends were unusually quiet the moment I caught up with them. When I asked what was wrong, they said they had some speed but thought maybe I should chill. I told them I'd be the judge of that and started shooting the stuff. I was one day out of jail and at it again!

Anxious for more kicks and highs, I went out with a cute hippy couple named Sheila and Bill, in order to smoke dope and drink beer. Bill had the cool car in town, a souped up Chevy Impala. We drove to the 'sand pits', a secluded place where we could party without being disturbed. Bill, who with Sheila, only did grass and alcohol, was so high that he laid rubber in front of Burger King. Sure enough, a policeman pulled us over. Having given Bill and Sheila my 'works' and 'drugs' to hide up front, I was pleasantly stoned and mellow, thinking this was Bill's problem, not mine. The cop approached the car and asked Billy where he'd been that night. He politely answered, "Just riding around, Sir."

Then he flashed his light on me and said something like, "Mr. Steiger, whatta you know!" This guy happened to be the biggest jerk on the Greenfield police force, which had it in for me. When he ordered me out of the car, I said "No. What's the problem?" He said that if I didn't, they would get a search warrant. I immediately said, "I haven't done anything. Go ahead!" But after thinking about it, I reluctantly got out, not wanting to draw attention to Bill and Sheila, since they had the 'stash' with them. I did this not knowing that the cops already knew I had a fat 'dubie' behind my ear. Suddenly the cop, who liked hassling me, reached behind my ear and pulled out a joint and held it in front of my face. He kept saying "We have you now! What have we here?" To which I abruptly answered, "Marijuana!" Then, in one quick swoop, I quickly grabbed the joint out of his hand and, after managing to collect enough saliva in an already dry mouth, swallowed it, choking! After telling Billy to get the hell outta there, they forcibly pushed me over to the curb and proceeded to beat my head against the sidewalk to dislodge the object. Failing to do so, they handcuffed me backwards so it would hurt more, threw me on the floor of the cruiser and began kicking and punching me all the way to the station.

Once there, they booked me on several charges. While this was occurring some of the cops must have urinated all over my cell because I found it everywhere!

The next morning, I went before the judge looking like a junkie out of dope: torn clothing, beaten up and hung over. The judge read the charges against me, which were: drunkenness, disorderly conduct and possession of marijuana. Then pausing, he said, "because the defendant ate the evidence, we have nothing to go on." The judge chuckled and everyone in the courtroom let out a roaring laugh! I was, however, fined $175.00 for the other two charges and if I couldn't pay the thirty-dollar minimum, I would go back to jail until I did. Fortunately for me, I had thirty-five, so life on the outside would go on.

About a month later, a bunch of us were pulled over while riding through town one night. I cringed when I saw Stockwell, a State Trooper who was friends with the Greenfield cop that liked giving me trouble, coming toward the car. I guess word was out to 'get Steiger'. There's really no need to mention all the times I was unnecessarily hassled, but this occasion deserves some explaining. As I expected, 'Statie Stockwell' let everyone else go, but cuffed me because he found a jack-knife in my back pocket. I was tripping my brains out and couldn't answer any of his questions. He took me on a 'hell ride', his lights flashing as he drove down the Mohawk Trail going about a hundred! I remember mumbling to him, "It's okay if you let me out here," and then he sped up more. He brought me in the holding cell where it was freezing cold. They didn't give me a blanket but half way through the night I was given one. I made my phone call to my ex-girlfriend, Holly, and she bailed me out. The remaining balance of my fine could not be paid by the due date, so I called my and told him about my situation and that I wanted to come back to Worcester. So he came out to Greenfield and paid off my fine. The police were extremely happy that I was finally leaving town. Now, I would be heading back to Eddie, Sue, Booky, Beany and the rest of the tribe.

Chapter 6

The New Crew

'I'm going to find me a wife,
A woman will fix my hurt.
As soon as I start to feel the pain,
We can bury it in the dirt.'

The return to Worcester was actually a welcome rest for me. I got a job and was just smoking weed. Slowly though, an addict gets bored and goes back to the chaos of the using life. I started sniffing the degreaser from the machine I operated for a rush. Quite often, my employer would send me home thinking I was sick. While walking around Elm Park one day, I noticed two teenagers, no older then sixteen, shivering on a bench. I asked them what the problem was and they said they were dope sick. I asked them if they knew where to cop. When they said yes, we were off to Kirby Street (a heavy drug dealing area) to buy some heroin. I bought a couple of 'big spoons' and gave them enough to get high and I did the rest. They had to carry me out of the house, thinking I was going to overdose. I gave them a number to call and a buddy came to pick me up. Heroin never left for long!

Eddie and Sue had no idea that I was shooting dope. Sue was working in a pizza shop and Eddie was doing odd jobs around Worcester. Even though I was living with them again, I didn't see them very much. I was eighteen-years old and though it was 1969, for me, 'the times were not a 'changing'.' I was given the chance to go to an outward-bound type school in New Hampshire to learn how to read and write better. When it was time to sign up, I brought Eddie with me and told them to take Eddie instead. I figured he had more of an opportunity them me to make good on it. I visited him once and learned he had been doing well in the program.

I tried using my 'almighty willpower' with drugs and alcohol. A few reds, a couple joints and a six-pack of beer would do my willpower great good. The only time I felt spiritual and comfortable without medicating myself was while playing drums. I fell in love with Ginger Baker, a double bass drummer with Jack Bruce and Eric Clapton, who was a well-known speed freak. I began getting more and more compliments on my playing. Eddie and Sue would come into my room and watch me practice.

As siblings, we were still close. Eddie was at the age where he would dare Sue and I to do this or that. I remember one winter day when he dared us to go outside and roll in the snow. After we refused, I told him he didn't have the guts to do it either. So he ran outside in his underwear, jumping up and down in the snow. While laughing our heads off, we locked the doors so he couldn't come inside. Finally, before he kicked the door down, I let him in. He was swearing and shaking at the same time. Sue almost wet her pants laughing so hard! I loved watching Sue laugh more than anything in the world. If you're reading this Eddie, sorry about that!

On Christmas, my father would perform his magic. Barbara, a schoolteacher, was also a talented painter, whose holiday artwork beautifully decorated the home. We had some good times and as will happen on occasion for an addict, things calmed down. But unless drugs are totally out of your life, serenity is always temporary.

'I was still smoking weed and being a week-end warrior.'
'The heroin was gone for the most part, but I was substituting'
'Again I was relying on will power.'

'I had no intention to stop, it was will power to slow down,
never to quit.'
'Quitting wasn't an option.'
'My quest was to achieve the perfect high, whether it be acid,
ludes or smack.'
My family knew I was drinking a lot, but they figured I just fit
into the 'family lineage'.
'Looking for answers and right-living
Would not change the suicide of my soul.
When you have nothing to lose,
The answers are easy to choose.'

I met a guy at work by the name of Al Purtle. I always
carried a pint of brandy on me and gave him a hit one-day.
After that, we went out for beers when our workday ended.
He told me he was in Vietnam and how many men he killed.
I told him about my 4F status and that I wasn't going to the
slaughterhouse which was taking so many lives and screwing up
so many people's heads. Al was one of those who would never be
the same again. I felt there were so many traps to fall into in this
country, that no one needed to go to Vietnam and kill people
and then get all screwed up!

Al Purtle and I became party pals, hanging out together,
going to bars and partying like there was no tomorrow. Al
seemed to have a death wish; he drank a lot more than I did. I
met a couple of his friends, Franny, another crazy party animal,
and Dennis Brown, a real hippie from California. We would
party over at Al's apartment constantly.

One time we were on a five-day binge and we were both
fired. I never told these guys about my heroin habit, but would
sneak out and cop a shoot in the bathroom or anywhere they
weren't. Al used to give me a hard time for always throwing up
whenever we partied—if he only knew. Franny asked me where
I was going one day and I was drunk enough to tell him. He
wanted to try it, but I said it probably wasn't a good idea. He
said he had two hundred dollars on him; it instantly became a
good idea. During this binge, Al came into the kitchen where

Dennis and I were drinking and made an announcement that he was going to pick up his new girlfriend and nobody was to go near her. We didn't care about her, until he made such a strong prohibition regarding our treatment of his woman. He actually generated interest by his demand. Ann would come over to the house and sit in the kitchen next to Al and not move all night. Every Friday night she did the same thing. One night I was going to the fridge to get a beer and she was sitting there by herself. I saw some grass sticking out of her pocketbook and proceeded to ask her to come party in the other room. I took her by the hand and she came in and partied. This proved my insanity. I was putting the make on Al's girl. We ended up lying on the couch all night and talked while Al sat across from us passed-out in the recliner. I really connected with Ann because she had a gentleness about her that was really endearing. I didn't care what Al said. I was going to get to know this woman better!

I then moved in with a friend of Al's whose name was Linda. My heroin use was around fifty dollars a day. Linda knew Ann well and used to ask me if I liked her. When I said sure, Linda told me to call Ann and so I did. Ann came over one day and we partied, smoking joints and drinking rum. Following that experience, she started coming over to see me more often.

Al came over to our place one night after I had taken some acid and asked me to go for a ride. By then Ann and Steve were in the back seat of the car. I climbed in front with Al and we roared off down the road. I looked at Ann and saw that she'd been crying. Al drove onto the highway and floored it, while mumbling something to himself about women! He yelled, "Let's all die, M-fer's!" and headed toward the guardrail. I screamed as loud as I could and right before we hit the rail, Al swerved back into the lane, laughing and swearing. We headed to the package store and then went back to Al's. We all needed a drink after that! I had no idea what was going to happen next, but when you're using you don't really look beyond the moment.

Al was across the room from me when he reached down and grabbed the quart bottle of rum at his feet. He gulped down the last of the contents, then winged it at my head. I ducked and the bottle smashed the wall behind me. He came at me with everything he had. I stood there without moving, not even raising my arms in defense. He put his fist through the plaster of the wall next to me and started screaming in my face like a drill sergeant. There was foam caked to the corners of his mouth and he was spitting at me. I stood there without budging, expressionless and stoic. I was waiting to feel his hands around my throat or a knife in my gut. Whatever the case, I knew this was the end of the line. Suddenly Al turned away and walked over to the fridge to get a beer. That was it! He stumbled into the living room and sat down and, from then on, never mentioned Ann and me again. In fact, he gave me a ride every now and then to pick her up.

Ann and I moved in together and after a year we were married by the Justice of the Peace at her parents' house. We were only twenty years old. But before our marriage, I finally broke down one night and told her I used heroin. She said she understood and that we would deal with it in time.

At a party in Al's apartment, Ann told me that she wanted to try heroin, but I said that wouldn't be a good thing to do. But she said if I didn't shoot her up she would have Dennis or some other guy do it, therefore, I agreed to do it. Her parents blame me for getting her hooked, but I knew if it wasn't me who hit her, one of the other guys would have done so. I felt she was safer getting it from me. Our married days turned into doing a bag of dope and then listening to the Moody Blues. Ann was from a very straight-laced family; her father was a Postmaster General; her mother the proverbial housewife. They had no idea about this life their daughter had entered.

Me, playing drums in a rock band, 1969.

Chapter 7

Family Matters

'I'm going to settle down,
But just not today.
I have not got it yet,
I do things the same ole way.'

Family life requires income, so I got a job at Norton's, one of the most prosperous factories in Massachusetts. Ann made out the application for me, since my writing was horrible. I leveled with the guy on the interview and told him I was newly married and wanted to settle down in the area. Ann had heard about signing up for low-income families who wanted to buy a house. We found a home we could purchase through this program in Oxford, Massachusetts, the birthplace of Clara Barton.

After we moved in, Ann asked me if I wanted children. I told her I was having a hard enough time taking care of myself, never mind any kid. She assured me it would be all right and so we had two children, three years apart. Dennis and Fran would still come over occasionally and do a bag of heroin, but for the most part, I was trying to chill out. I knew I needed my job at Norton's and that there was no quicker way to lose it than to be hanging out with guys like Dennis and Fran.

It was around this time that I got a call from Eddie saying Dad was in a major bike accident near his house in nearby Spencer, Massachusetts. He had hit a tree going about fifty.

When I arrived at the hospital nobody but the nurses were in the room. He was a total mess, with tubes and IV's everywhere. It seems that they were having trouble keeping the brace on one of his broken arms. They even tied his arm to the side of the bed so he couldn't reach down and take it off. What they didn't know was that Dad is a magician who kept finding ways to get untangled.

Dad had been living alone at the camp and was in the process of divorcing Barbara. When they finally released him from the hospital, I took him back to Oxford to nurse him back to health. He was frail and weak, sounding like he'd given up on life. After a few good months though, he was up and around, working with wood again and building different things. I continued to stay in his life, helping him fix up the camp while he healed.

The domestic life was becoming attractive to me. Ann had out first child, Jesse, when I was twenty-four. I was in the delivery room when she gave birth and found it to be one of the most incredible experiences of my life! Nothing can make everything in this dumb world seem so irrelevant than staring at your own child. I ran down the hallway of the hospital, yelling and screaming like I'd won the lottery! To me, it was as if I had.

I was still drinking and drugging, of course, but had learned how to play the game. I began feeling lazy and bloated, overweight and flabby. I remember sitting in my living room smoking my brains out, watching Rocky. In doing that, I decided to try to get into shape. Beginning with one mile jogs around my neighborhood, I started becoming more and more interested in getting healthy, even stopping to smoke dope. I recall watching the runner Bill Rogers on television. He became my mentor, so I tried to do everything he did. I heard he ate pizza for breakfast, so that's what I did, too. I wanted to get back to the way I felt while running track in high school. The only trouble, I wallowed in self-pity when I didn't do well. I was constantly beating myself up for not being perfect. This attitude made me increase my alcohol consumption.

I learned that there was a popular road race in Worcester

called Charlie's Surplus Ten-Miler and that Bill Rogers would
be there. I called my father to tell him I was going to run a race
in Worcester. To my surprise he came and watched his son do
well. This was another highlight of my life, having my father
attend an event in which I was involved. My wife was there with
Jesse, now four years old. By now, I was twenty-eight years old
and had come a long way physically. I ran the race in the sixty-
three minutes and finished in the top ten percentile. My name
was in the local paper and this got me back into the running
life. My nickname at work was always 'Staggering Don' for my
unique way of slumbering around the shop. But after the race,
they called me the 'Runner' instead.

My drinking was picking up around this time. It always
seemed to be—train hard, play hard! One of our neighbors,
a real nice man named Dick, used to time me when I ran.
Physically I was in my prime, but mentally I was using more
pills and alcohol to escape reality. Then I pulled a hamstring
and was on crutches for three months. The doctor gave me a
prescription for Percodan. I began my pill popping again.

Ann was miserable, throwing stuff at me and begging me
to hit her. Some nights I did. I saw the battling of my parents
reflected in my own home. Ann then proceeded to tell me she
was pregnant again. She had our second child, a beautiful girl we
named Amy. Again, I thought my life was now going to be the
ever-lasting peace for which I had always yearned.

It was around this time that Ann answered the phone
one night and told me it was a nurse asking for the son of
Sue Steiger. It had been years since I spoke to anyone even
remotely involved in my mother's life. I reluctantly took the
call and found out my mother had been shot point-blank in
the stomach. The nurse said my mother needed a place to
recuperate, a place where someone could take good care of her.
It seemed Eddie, Sue and my father had already refused to take
her in and I told the nurse neither could I. I felt disgusted that
things had gone so badly in my life with Mom that I could not
agree to nurse her back to health. I just didn't have the desire to
let her back into my life again.

Shortly after this, Ann threw a Christmas party at our house. Our neighbor, Dick, brought a guest with him named Jesse and I instantly knew he was high on heroin. When I asked, he told me where he got it, so we crept out the back door and went to cop. That night set up the compulsion for drugs and I was off and running, so to speak, for the next week. Now I had a new partner in crime, one who was young, and vibrant and full of energy. He loved the drug scene practically as much as the drugs themselves. We started robbing drug stores at night, driving around during the day with a trunk full of drugs. My wife figured I was on a booze binge and would snap out of it in a few days.

I was beginning to give up on the life I had created. I remember taking the cross off my neck that Aunt Pat had given me in the prison hospital and mailing it to her, because it made me feel too shameful all the time. One night, after a heated argument, I called a friend of Ann's to ask her what she thought I should do. I didn't want to lose my family and realized that these fights had to end. I would not hurt Ann, but I did use force and slapped her on occasion. She told me I should go into 'detox' to get off drugs. I went to Adcare Hospital in Worcester to clean up for a couple of weeks.

I left that place worse than when I went in, they gave me more drugs than I was taking on the outside; Methadone in the day and tranquilizers at night. I started hiding the night pills in the curtain hinges. I hated feeling like a zombie and thought this place was a joke. I stayed for two weeks and had a bag of heroin waiting for me when I left. This was the beginning of the lowest point of my life and I didn't even have a clue! I was so strung-out that I did something I thought I would never do—sell my drums!

Things got bad real quickly. Jesse was still drugging and would swing by my work, take my order and meet me afterwards well supplied. Slowly I began getting back to daily using. I felt like my life was coming to an end and it scared the hell out of me. I went to my sister, in whom I had not confided in a long time, telling her I was so 'screwed up'! She just looked at me with these sad eyes and said she didn't know how to help me. Without any help, it kept getting worse and worse.

My stealing was becoming more serious, in that, I would go into the Norton plant at night with a security uniform on, looking like one of the guards. I'd bring the guard in the booth a cup of coffee, mumbling something, and he'd let me walk by. I proceeded to make my way over to the diamond-cutting wheels and fill my bag. My 'fence' would give me three -hundred a pop for the wheels and that would buy a lot of dope. I was steeling everything I could get my hands on. The cutting wheels were always in high demand in the auto body shops and I never had any trouble getting rid of them. The fear of getting caught was increasing and in a weird way I almost wished I would. I stole over $200,000.00 worth of materials from Norton's and it all went into my arm.

One night, after work, I over-dosed on some bad stuff, after I made a nice big hit for myself. I had been up for days celebrating my birthday and copped some drugs off a guy I didn't know. It was some dude who hung out on the street corner where I worked. By the grace of God, I didn't give Ann the same 'burn'! I am not sure what I put into my veins to this day; rat poison, horse tranquilizer, whatever. The room began getting fuzzy and I got 'bad' sick, not the 'good' sick of heroin. Ann rushed me to the hospital and, on the way, went by my place of work. In a move that can only describe her character, she was demanding my money back (which she did get), while I was dying in the car, and also trying to figure out what he had given me. But he himself didn't even know.

When she was done screaming at this guy, she took me to Memorial Hospital in Worcester and helped me walk into the emergency room. The admitting nurse asked her what was wrong and she frantically said, "He overdosed on some bad stuff" and then dumped me into a wheel chair. I collapsed momentarily, then woke up scared...kicking and screaming! They strapped me down and shouted at me, "What have you taken?" But I didn't know, nor did Ann. I somewhat remember a cop asking me repeatedly what I had taken. I heard them but could not answer. They got frustrated and left and finally, so did Ann. I lay on a table for what seemed like three hours before they made me drink what I think was ipecac. It was supposed to make me puke. Afterwards, I started tripping out, seeing angels appearing from the ceiling. I saw old friends come in and talk to me, believing they were actually there. When they asked me to party with them, I told them I couldn't 'cause I was in the hospital.

Following that strange ordeal, I, at least thought about chilling out again. Jesse left for Boston to buy drugs and the turmoil calmed down a little. I got a band together, thinking it would break my obsession to use. My brother Eddie, was already working in a popular band around Worcester called Zonkeraz. A few friends and I met Eddie for dinner one night. I introduced him to Barbara, one of my musician friends. They hit it off well and were later married. They even had twins and Ann and I would go over to see our nieces, Debby and Kathy, all the time. The drugs came back into my life slowly, as they always do, when you think you can use socially. Ann's habit was also increasing, but all in all, with the kids, the house and the band, I was keeping busy and feeling pretty good!

My first child, Jesse, and myself, Cape Cod, Massachusetts,
early 1970's.

Detox located in the building on the right.

Worcester State Hospital Detox Unit (my 5th or 6th visit).

In shape and running in the annual Charlie's Surplus 'Mother's Day' Ten-miler (time 63:11) in 1980.

Chapter 8

The Walls Come Tumbling Down

'It was only a matter of distance.
It was only a matter of time.
Until I've learned my lesson,
These walls I'll stay behind.'

Around this time, my friend Jesse came back into town. He looked good and told me he scored big in Boston. We walked around my backyard, smoking joints and taking it easy. Jesse knew the drugs had him. We used to laugh at the insanity. That's what they mean by the 'bonds' created through addiction. We were literally blood brothers, in this sick heroin war together. Nobody wants to do a drug every day of their life just to function, whether heroin or alcohol. I was developing another bad habit. Every time things got crazy, I would check into a detox for twenty-one days to chill out. Ann, now also struggling with her own heroin habit, would do the same. Norton's was and amazingly hard place to get fired from, so I barely kept my job in tact. I was still stealing all kinds of stuff from there, filling my fence's house with all sorts of material.

I kept thinking to myself that the family life was helping me to hang on. I truly loved Amy and Jesse. Being a father was a really good feeling and had a lot of responsibility. Jesse and I would do stretching exercises and sit ups, then jog around the block slowly. He was a natural for running! We enjoyed laughing and joking together. To be a father with a son was a proud and exciting experience! I loved spending time with Amy too. I read to her stories like 'Cat in the Hat' books and played cards with her. Amy loved the games 'War' and 'Old Maid'. We laughed and shared special moments that I will always treasure.

I remember dropping off Amy for her recital practice and then driving to Worcester to cop heroin. I always planned on making it back in time to pick her up. She was only five, and often times, I would be anywhere from one-half to one hour late. She'd be sitting there by herself crying. I'll never forget the horrible feeling of being dope sick and seeing my own flesh and blood, my loving, helpless Amy's eyes seeing me. I felt so full of shame and humiliation that my heart was torn from my chest!

It was frustrating trying to be a good father while being pulled apart by my drug abuse. I was screaming inside and hated myself for being this way, but I tried covering it up with drugs. I wanted to be a father to my kids in the best possible way, but my soul belonged to the drugs, and the more I did the further I got!

I felt shame and remorse and pain in my heart for my children because I was being pulled out of my home in order to cop. Once again, it got to the point of just 'using' to feel normal. Whenever I didn't have it I was awfully sick, kind of like having the flu, and you know you're going to get worse if you don't get something quick! I kept saying to myself:

> 'One last time,
> This is the last time.
> One more time.
> This is the last one.'

Doing this to my children was like watching someone you love drowning at your fingertips: helpless!

I often took Jesse's paper route money so I could use it to cop. He also had a 'sixth sense' when I was sick and would give me his 'tip' money from the paper route.

I can honestly say that never in my lifetime could I ever

make something like this right! I had been blessed with two of the most perfect children in the world and I was blowing it...real bad!

One night while sitting in the kitchen having a beer, my daughter Amy on my lap, some guys in suits came in an announced they were looking for 'Mr. Don Steiger'. After telling them that I was Mr. Don Steiger, they identified themselves as FBI and placed me under arrest for 'grand larceny'. Then they searched me in front of Amy, which I found humiliating. I asked if they would let me bring my daughter home first and they agreed. I was really dope sick and needed to get some heroin in me. After eight hours of interrogation, I told the FBI that if they gave me money to cop I would tell them everything they wanted to know. Agreeing, they gave me the money and sent me home. The next day, after I got high, I was so moronic that I walked into work as if nothing had happened. They called my name over the loud speaker, ordered me to clean out my locker, fired me, and said to me that if they ever saw me around there again I would be going to jail for a long time. I drove off and traded my car in to the dope man for three bags. I knew I was going down and I was going to get high!

My new hobby became shoplifting. I would go into Zayer's or Spag's and fill my coat with anything I could carry. It was 1983. I was thirty-three years old and down and out in Worcester, Massachusetts. I got arrested for shoplifting and now had a definite jail sentence awaiting me. I shot so many drugs that the veins in my arm gave out, forcing me to use my feet and legs to shoot dope. I called Spectrum House because I knew I had to get help and fast. At first, they kept telling me that no beds were available, but finally, they told me to come in. This was my fifth detox.

My father, whom I visited once and a while in Spencer, brought me in. He took pictures of all the drug paraphernalia in my house. He told the admitting nurse to do whatever it takes, including tying me to the bed. They informed him I had a constitutional right to leave if I chose to. He then started to panic, but I re-assured him I would stay. I started experiencing the worst withdrawal symptoms I could remember. It was ninety-three degrees in there and I though I was going to pass out. I told the nurse to either help me kick this addiction or shoot me. After my father left, I had to once again go through the long process of being admitted, with all the paperwork, blood tests and de-licing shower. The nurse asked me certain family information such as how old were my children. I told her my son was seven and a half and my daughter was five, and they were the best kids in the world! But obviously, the heroin was winning out over the love of my children. The doctor who came to give me my physical knew me by first name. "You made it back, Donnie," he said stoically. I told him that this time it was going to be different, like he had never heard that line before. He examined my arm and asked me how big my habit had gotten. I said around $100 to $200 a day, which included barbiturates and intravenous drugs. You have to get real honest with the doc because the withdrawal can kill you if you lie to him. I smoked a butt, then ran to the bathroom and threw-up for a long time. I felt like there were bugs crawling all over me. You might say I had the 'heebie-geebies, woops and jingles'! It was 12:30 pm and I had been there for three hours.

Spectrum House detox used methadone to wean you off the dope. It is a strong drug that replaces the addiction to heroin. They would then wean you off the methadone so that you could, supposedly, get on with your life. I knew of very few addicts who got clean and stayed clean using this method. I didn't see anyone around me making it, so I had little hope for myself. Three and a half hours and still no methadone; I was losing it! One of the most degrading things was seeing the second shift nurses and counselors again. They gave you that look which said, "Oh Donnie, not again." I finally got my methadone at 3:30 pm, six hours after I had arrived. I received 30mgs crushed up in applesauce. The first does did nothing for me. I was still puking and shaking. The nurses saw I was still out of it and called the doctor at home. He okayed another dose and this one stopped the sickness for a while, at least. I finally lay down to rest and was awakened every hour on the hour for my blood pressure and pulse. The nurses wanted to make sure I made it through the first two nights.

The next morning I managed a little toast with jelly and some juice. I was made the 'checker' on the second day, checking all the patients. At night I couldn't sleep because the voices in the 'rubber room' downstairs were loud as hell. One of the counselors said only about 3 out of 25 would stay sober a year. He said that in all likelihood, it would not be any of us. I took this as a challenge, a personal goal. I highly suggest it to any counselor reading this that telling a bunch of addicts they can't do something is the best way to make them do it! There was one opening for long-term care and I took it. Although this was detox number 5, it was the first long term one for me. I packed my bags and waited to leave for the other facility. Meanwhile Ann came by with our son Jesse and daughter Amy. It was quite an emotional scene; I was crying, Ann was crying and our kids were crying. I told my kids that daddy was sick and needed to go on a little trip and would be back in no time. Ann said she loved me and not to worry about a thing. It's funny, because I was more afraid than I had ever been in my life because the scariest part was doing something about my addiction. I'll never understand how the addict's mind works.

One day I was called into the office to see my doctor, counselor and nurse. They asked me what I wanted to do and I asked them for some suggestions. Let's see, long-term care — 18 months at Spectrum. This was a huge block of time but despite my doubts, I had already agreed to do the time. Ann and my friend, Jesse, said they would take care of the house and the kids. Anyway this would certainly help my jail time. The short-term treatment program never worked because I never worked it, I just did not get it period. My head would start to clear up, but when the feelings would start to plague me, my self-esteem went down the toilet. After the drugs were out of my system, I would always become vulnerable and scared. The drugs masked everything, but slowly the drugs didn't work. I knew the answer might be long-term. But in the back of every addict's mind is that there must be a way to go than a life without any drugs in it.

On day eleven of detox, I was taken off methadone and shipped to Spectrum long-term care. I was sick and depressed. Driving up there, I felt like I was being brought to an exorcism. The death of Don the Addict had begun!

Myself (strung out, flabby and overweight) and Jesse (7).

Myself and Amy (5) at her dance recital, 1982.

Picture of my drugs and syringes taken by my father, days after
I entered treatment, June 28, 1984.

Going In...

I sat in the admittance room and noticed these strange
souls shuffling along the floor with signs around their necks.
One guy had a gigantic cigarette dangling from his neck, a rope
coming out of the ash ran up his chest and behind his neck. It
turns out that the man was caught smoking in the bathroom,
something no one was supposed to do. This meant he had to
wear that giant cigarette wherever he went for a week. Later on,
I would know how he felt, for it was to be my turn at wearing
that hideous contraption. Another time, I saw a man entering
a room next to mine and announcing, "Excuse me, my name is
Jim and I can't be trusted." Everyone in the room responded,
"Okay." This poor soul got caught stealing sugar packets from
the coffee room.

Whenever someone broke the rules, they would undergo
what was called the 'hair-cut'. This was when a patient was
brought up before the counselors and then allowed to be torn

apart by their fellow patients. Again, I would learn more about this later during my stay.

All this information was given to me by one of the counselors, a big and tall black man having the name Hydrick. Though he was huge and tough looking, he had this calm, serene disposition that made me sick. He filled me in on the rules for those patients who didn't go by the rules. For people on 'learning experience', there was no talking, joking or laughing between them except at designated times. Neither was there to be 'drug talk' among the patients. If you kept breaking the rules after a learning experience you were gone the next time they 'cleaned house'. Those addicts who couldn't follow the rules consistently were sent back to the streets. Since I learned all this the first day, I can't believe I stayed!

For the first thirty days, I had someone with me twenty-four hours a day. This was supposedly to cut down on suicides. This silent 'suicide guard' even followed me to the bathroom. The withdrawal process was unbelievable. Heroin replaces you body's natural ability to create endorphins and when the heroin was gone, I simply didn't have any! My eyelids even hurt when I blinked. My nerves were also shot. I remember my hand coming up and slapping my face uncontrollably or sleeping and having my arm, then my leg, suddenly jump-to without any warning.

The first three months went by a minute at a time and I was crying everyday. There was a paradox going on in my head: I hated it there, but then again, I felt like I was in a safe place for the first time in my life. I started pulling myself away from the people who were always getting me into trouble. If I was going to go through all of this, I was going to stay sober. Every morning at breakfast, I would sit by myself and eat, still shaking and quivering. I would start crying uncontrollably, the dammed up emotions of years coming back.

I was CRYING because the babysitters hurt me and my brother and sister!

I was CRYING because I watched my dog Rocket get shot!

I was CRYING because I mailed my cross back to Aunt Pat!

I was CRYING because heroin sucks and ruins your insides!

My emotions were flying so high that I would get these rebellious jags. Three times a week I would see Hydrick and be always mad as hell, ranting and raving about something. He would always just sit there, hands folded on his little potbelly. "So Mr. Steiger. What is the problem today?" I would reply in the kindest possible way, "Blank you! Blank this place and blank you too!" Sometimes I would spit on the floor, storming out of his office like a madman on a mission. Smiling, Hydrick would say, "So, Mr. Steiger, you're choosing not to face yourself today, that's all right. Go wash dishes in the pan and we'll try again another day. In the pan, Steiger. Two weeks in the pan!" This meant a 'learning experience' for me. I was scrubbing pans all day, every day. When I wasn't scrubbing pans, I was scrubbing floors with a wire brush. This 'weirdo woman' named Linda always wandered around the floor/unit screaming at me," You are a loser! A loser!" I would sit there crying and praying from the bottom of my soul to have the power not to hit her. One time I got angry with Hydrick about something and threw a piece of cantaloupe at him in the recreation room, missing his head by inches as it bounced off the coffeepot!

Now it was time for my haircut. I went to Hydrick's office and knocked on his door. It went something like this:

"Who is that?"

"Donald Steiger, sir."

"Who?"

"Donald Steiger, sir."

"Get in here, Steiger!"

I entered the room and there was Hydrick sitting in the corner of his office. Two appointed patients were always chosen to give the haircuts. You were required to stand at attention while those appointed sat side by side in front of you. Then they would begin screaming at you one by one, sometimes together. If you acted out of order, you were gone.

"I suppose you want to go back to jail, Mr. Steiger!"

"I suppose you want to go back on the street and die a miserable junkie!"

"What about your kids, you selfish loser?"

"Don't you care about your family, you stupid idiot?"

Then Hydrick would conclude with a little encouragement; "Don, you are worth saving. But you have to get up and start living life the way it is supposed to be lived. Get out of here and start shaping up your sorry self!"

Myself with Amy and Jesse at Spectrum House on visiting day—five months sober.

Keeping On

"Oh God, what does punishment have to do with serenity?"
—Ask Jackie Robinson

I was only allowed to say, thank you. Some patients started defending themselves or copping an attitude. If you did this, you were thrown out and had to come back and do it all over again.

One day I got caught smoking and was sentenced to the 'giant cigarette'. I had to see Hydrick with this ridiculous thing around my neck. "So, Steiger, you thought you were different. That you could smoke anywhere! You've been here three months and come in and tell me to get lost while you go out and sneak cigarettes! What do you suggest we do?"

I had no answer. I wore that cigarette for three weeks. I was also afraid that they were going to kick me out of there. The only time you could take the cigarette off was upstairs in the sleeping room. At the end of the third week, I took the stupid cigarette off my neck one night and smashed it against the wall. Of course, the thing didn't break, but the news spread quickly that I had freaked out again. The next day, I traded in the cigarette for a sign. A giant paper poster which read; 'Instead of dealing with my feelings in appropriate ways, I choose to act like a baby and dump them all over the floor.' I wore this sign twenty-four hours a day for weeks.

Testing The Limits

'When will you break
Persecuted and being humiliated
See what he does
Carrying the weight of cutting words
That fall into my soul, the pain I
Cannot bear.'

In my opinion, the only reason they didn't expel me is

because I would go into Hydrick office and beg him to help me. I told him I couldn't control my emotions and it scared me. I was slowly opening up to this wise black man who listen patiently to my pathetic outbursts. After the cigarette-throwing incident, there was a break in the sickness. I started to realize there just might be a way out of this hell. It took six months to come to that conclusion.

A Hispanic by the name of Raoul came into rehab around this time. He always cried and wandered the floor alone. I gave him a big hug and told him that I cared about him. It was the first time I would learn that helping others is the most important part of staying sober. I showed him the ropes and told him everything would be all right if he just hung in there. I'm not sure I believed what I told him myself, but I still did anyway! Recently, I got a call from Raoul telling me that he had been sober for over thirteen years and wanted to thank me again for my help.

One night I was sent upstairs by the counselors to check on Billy, a convicted armed robber who was staying at Spectrum House instead of jail. Billy was a good friend, teaching me more about how to read. For the first time in my life, I read a book from beginning to end. It was 'Jonathan Livingston Seagull', my all time favorite. When I saw Billy, he was smoking a cigarette, a no-no upstairs. The staff smelled the smoke and asked me who was smoking. I knew if I didn't get honest with them I was in trouble. I told them it was Billy and they sent him back to jail. I became angry and depressed after they did this to someone I liked, but I also realized that I couldn't lie anymore about things either.

Ann's mother Rose began bringing the kids on weekends and would drop them off so we could spend the day together. When they left with her, I could hear Jesse and Amy screaming 'not to leave Daddy behind'. I remember seeing their faces in the back window full of pain and anguish. Thanks again, heroin!

I would now like to mention my first spiritual awakening in recovery. This was probably the most important moment in my life thus far. I was still a punk, not playing by the rules and thinking I was somehow above the law of the land. One day I walked upstairs and found Raoul on his knees praying in Spanish. He got up and told me he felt much better. I asked him how praying could possibly make him feel better. He told me that every morning he asked God to remove his character defects and obsession to use drugs and alcohol and to turn his life and will over to the care of God as he understood Him. I did not fully understand what he meant by 'turning it over', but I did know that my will and my pride, as I understood it, was not working and I needed something else to take their place. I went to my room and knelt down by my bed and asked God to relieve my obsession for drugs and help me with my character defects (whatever that meant), which were causing me so much pain. I felt, from the depths of my soul, this warm comfortable feeling that ran through my body, making it feel better than a bag of dope ever did! It filled me with such positive energy that I was totally enraptured. I felt a perfect acceptance of life and the universe. I wandered downstairs and decided to start cleaning the dirtiest part of the kitchen and was rather content doing it. Hydrick came out and saw me whistling while going to town cleaning and gave me this strange stare! I was definitely out of character. Looking back at this day, it becomes more and more important to realize that the spiritual breakthrough began with me on my knees.

I would lie awake in bed at night thinking differently about things. I wondered about this 'program of action' they were talking about in recovery meetings. I knew I had to jump in completely or fall by the wayside totally. I started getting up half an hour before everyone else in order to shower. I was in charge of the three travel vans, checking the oil and writing down the mileage, etc. My responsibilities increased, but my serenity was growing at the same time! I was still having panic attacks and bouts of anxiety, but I discovered that praying every morning was certainly more effective than anything else...drugs included!

One time I felt very angry inside and was ready to leave

this place. I packed up my things and was sitting on the front porch when a fellow patient, named Tom came out on to the porch. He asked me where I was going and I told him I was out of there. He threw his cigarette down and grabbed me by the shoulders and said, "Donnie, I love you and I don't love a lot of people. This is the only place for people like us. Give it one more day." I saw tears in his eyes and never before knew this kind of sincerity in my life. I also knew in the back of my mind that if I stepped off the porch, I would die! It was as simple as that. I cried in his arms, letting go of the welled up emotion I had carried for so many years. I agreed to stay for one more day. That's all an addict needs to do, stay one more day! Tom is still around today, and I will be forever grateful for his help.

So my spiritual awakening was not a full and mighty exaltation into peace. There was a battle going on and I was in boot camp. I had now been in treatment for seven months and my life consisted mostly of cleaning house and attending meetings. A whole book could be written about these groups. If you could imagine 75 addicts living under the same roof, you would easily see the potential for some interesting moments. It was 1984 and the Aids epidemic had just started gaining momentum. Two other diseases, Hepatitis B and C were also killing addicts. I tested negative for Aids but positive for Hepatitis B. I never got sick, but I do remember being unusually tired for a while. Hepatitis B attacks the liver and I am fortunate the disease was arrested in only a short time.

Back to the groups...the whole idea behind group was to air out any resentment you had toward other patients. You would book a haircut with a patient and confront that person with your resentment(s) in group, getting it all out in the open. There was no acting out in the groups, meaning you couldn't just say anything. But you were allowed to yell and scream, channeling your anger at whatever or whoever made you angry. Boy did it feel good to get angry sometimes. We were divided into four groups, which were held in different rooms: the main dining room or the recreation room. The rules were you could yell and scream but you couldn't threaten anyone or make any kind of sexual gestures toward people. The counselors themselves got involved in the groups and would participate in the activities. Despite my change of attitude, I was still in a lot of pain and felt remorse for my children. Besides my personal pain, there were just some people in my group who drove me crazy. There was one guy, named Red, who always sat in my group. He had red hair and red eyes and red skin, hence the name. Anyway, Red would always confront this other guy, Jerry, at the table. Jerry would go to reply and Red would scream at the top of his lungs. More than once, Red's false teeth came flying out of his mouth. The funniest part was that he never missed a stride when yelling, rambling on and on! Basically speaking, you couldn't get out of your chair or touch anyone but they let you verbally kill each other instead.

While at Spectrum House, I was going to school. My teacher worked with me on a one-to-one basis, helping me improve my spelling. I had already failed my GED a few times but Tom, a lawyer from Boston, as well as a resident at Spectrum, kept talking me into trying again. So, between Tom and Hydrick, that's exactly what I intended to do.

It was my ninth month and I shared with my group that my wife's visits were becoming less frequent. Hydrick told me to check out the situation at home and see if I wanted to return there once I completed the program. He gave me a day pass to go home. I missed my kids so much that I cried in their arms for ten minutes. I immediately saw evidence that Ann was smoking dope and doing heroin. I asked her if she would put down the drugs if I came home. She was indignant and told me she'd never change her ways for anyone and that I was the addict who'd left home, not her. I asked her if she was choosing drugs over me. All she said was, "I'm not going to pay for your mistakes or give up anything." In the end, she let me know that it was her choice if she wanted to pick a drug over me.

When I returned to Spectrum House, I shared this with the group. I just couldn't believe Ann would do this to me. I guess I imagined she would follow me right into the door of recovery, now I know it seldom works out that way. The months were rolling by and I had made it through one year. I must say that I saw a thousand different faces come and go in one year. Most of them didn't make it passed the first couple of weeks. I began to see how blessed I was to have painfully stuck it out during those first few horrible months. I began to see I was worthy of recovery and regardless of my miserable upbringing. I was capable of getting beyond this unhappy period of my life. I also realized, just like the time I lent a hand to Raoul, that I could help other addicts who were suffering with addiction to alcohol and drugs. Little did I realize then, my heart was starting to mend. I was actually thinking beyond my emotions, something I had never done before.

As part of treatment, I was doing insulation work ten to eleven hours a day, which included having to walk five or six miles each way. Working was an important aspect of the program because it was used to instill the necessary self-discipline needed to hold down a job by staying clean and sober.

By now I was doing insulation work and I remember receiving my first paycheck. I brought the check to the bank and opened an account, keeping $50 for the week and putting the rest in savings. What a great feeling I had doing the right thing! I kept working and saving and while I was doing this, a fellow graduate from the house, named Danny, came to visit me. He was a musician and wanted to know if I would like to buy a Ludwig drum set. I instantly told him yes and that I could pay for it now but couldn't get it until I finished treatment. Looking over my financial statement that I had to turn in to Hydrick each week, I knew he would not be happy. I ran into his office at the last minute and put my record book on his desk. Halfway up the stairs I heard his voice echo through the hall. "Mr. Steiger! Come here now!" I entered his office with my head down. He asked me on what had I spent the $65. I told him a set of used drums. Then he asked me, "Do you want to go back to jail you liar?" After telling him how important music was to me, he ordered me to give them back to Danny for a refund. So I said that I would. A week later, Hydrick asked if I had given back the drums and I said to him, in all honesty, that I hadn't.

The next night we had a house meeting. The head counselor, Tom, opened up the meeting by saying, "Is everybody happy to be here?" Seventy-five heads nodded yes. Then he said, "We have an issue concerning Don Steiger. Please stand Don." I was angry with Hydrick for having Tom single me out in front of the whole house. Tom asked if I had purchased a drum set a couple of weeks before. I said yes while staring sternly at Hydrick. Then Tom announced to the others that I had been in treatment for 14 months and that I would not be going home to my wife because of her drug use. He turned to me and said, "Don, you keep those drums. It's all you have right now." While Tom moved on to the next item of business, Hydrick looked at me and gave me a wink. After all this, I cried in relief!

When my eighteen months were up, it was time for me to move on. I made arrangements to rent a room in Hopkington for $150 a month. It felt strange on my last day there waiting to leave the place I had at first hated: those hard to deal with patients, Hydrick, Tom, the giant cigarette, etc. But this was the next step in my journey, something I had to take slowly. The next day before I left, Hydrick just looked at me and said, "I had better see your face at the after care meetings or I'll hunt you down." he then turned and walked down the hall. I loved that man more than any other human being in my entire life!

On the outside, I maintained my job of installing insulation and was glad to have something to keep me busy. Since it was a new chapter in my life, I was very apprehensive about the challenges that lay ahead. This uncertainty made me pray a lot each day because I knew I could not succeed alone.

The rooming house in Hopkington was really a nice and quiet place to live. I met a woman on one of the job-sites by the name of Lynn whom I asked out to dinner. When she said yes, I was pretty psyched! She was a great friend to me because she had a great passion for life and old-fashioned views. We painted her garage and took walks in the country. We also enjoyed holding hands and talking about music. I felt like a high school kid again. When I picked up my drum set from Danny, I practiced everyday in the cellar. I had my musical energy back! I even went to some nightclubs to hear various bands, feeling no desire to drink. I loved to dance and would have a great time without drugs or booze. My God had placed a neutral feeling in me regarding those two substances!

The toughest part for me was learning how to be alone. I would eat dinner by myself a lot and wonder if was going to be that way forever. But I also realized that my life was now a blank piece of paper and I could draw anything I wanted on it. I had this blind faith in God, believing He would take care of me and let me rise above these false feelings of loneliness. I also knew I needed to get back and forth to Spectrum House to participate in the after-care meetings. Hydrick informed me that I would be receiving my diploma the following month at the annual graduation ceremony. There were six of us who were scheduled to receive a certificate for eighteen months of clean time. Six out of thousands, it was mind-blowing! While waiting that month out, two of the six would start using again and one would die of an overdose.

This was definitely one of the strangest emotional periods of my life. I was working five days a week in my present job as an insulation installer plus being a 'demolition' man, tearing down old structures with a sledge hammer and crow-bar. On weekends I did construction jobs for extra money since I had to pay child support and restitution for the things I had taken from Norton's. In my spare time, I played drums whenever I got bored, eventually forming a band called Side Two. We played in various clubs and formed a group of other sober musicians called Artists in Recovery. I had fun playing and felt like I was beginning to live life again. I continued the after-care with Hydrick and would tell him about my state of confusion. When I wasn't in after-care, I ate alone, slept alone and cried alone. Sometimes after work I would go to Spectrum House and just sit on the porch and bawl. No one said a word to me. No one kicked me out. Thank God for that place!

The effect on my emotional life after using drugs for so

many years was severe. I lost months of my life in which I have no memory of what happened. The road back was going to be a long one, but I was told that with one day at a time it was possible. One of the addicts with whom I used drugs, Tom, moved in with my wife. Ann was still using heroin and did not want me around. Most of the time when I went to visit the kids she would keep me from seeing them. I never had the opportunity to see them for the holidays; not Christmas, not New Year's, not Easter, not even for their birthdays!

My graduation ceremony following an 18-month treatment program at Spectrum House, June, 1987 (postponed earlier).

Myself on the drums during an 'Artists in Recovery'
performance, 1989.

The Long Road Home
'The God I would choose if I turned it all over
What's happening now, will I stay sober? '

Dear Jesse and Amy,

I haven't had a chance to talk to either of you, so I want
both of you to know that you are in my prayers and that I love
you and am grateful to that I have you. I know it's been rough.
For a long time I have been thinking how I have not been there
for you. Above all else, I am sorry for this. I want you to know
that you are welcome in my home anytime.

I want to talk to you about change. Change can sometimes be difficult but when you think about it, we are always changing one way or another. The biggest difficulty in change is the fear that it brings. I want you to know that what has happened in my life before this great change has nothing to do with you. I took a lot of blame for my parents' behavior and felt empty inside because of it. I felt inadequate all my life and found drugs and alcohol to kill the pain, IT DIDN'T WORK! This is my change, but I want to talk about your change. How you deal with change will have a lot to do with how happy you'll be in this life.

The message I want you to take is that the right kind of change is good. I know I had to leave you to go get help and that change was probably very traumatic for you. I did this not to hurt you (I never did anything to hurt you) but to SAVE MY LIFE. I understand the emptiness and shame you must have felt about me. You became victims of my circumstances.

Love yourselves and put yourselves first. Amy, you are a beautiful and smart woman who is going places. You have a lot to offer people because you are caring and compassionate. I hear it when I talk to you on the phone—that you are a truly exceptional person! Jesse, you are also doing awesome and working hard. Follow your dreams and never give up. Be positive. Whenever you feel negative emotions like anger, jealousy and resentment ask God to take them away instantly. We have the power to change our thinking. We never have to blame others for our own lives. All my life I pointed the finger at others. I had to stop this in order to survive. Allow God to work everything out for you and wonderful things will happen!

I would also like to say something about opportunity. Opportunities in life will be available to you, but it won't always come to you. You must go after what you want and ask God for His will to be done, not yours. Jesse, when you don't talk to me very much that usually means something is up, right? You can call me anytime with any problem—remember this always!

About relationships: we do not own anyone and if you truly love someone, empower them to be free. I have lost a lot of love in my life because I tried to control my partner, since I was fearful and insecure. Let yourself love and be loved! It is the only thing that's real in life; that's worthwhile. Life is a learning experience. It is not about arriving anywhere or getting things. It is the journey. You NEVER arrive.

I give my problems to God and He takes care of them. I am truly a free man. I am fifty and feel like I'm twenty.

For you, Amy, follow your dreams too and explore your options. God will always be with you no matter where you go. Seek and you will find. Knock and the door will be open to you. For anyone who asks receives.

I love and miss both of you so much! I realize you have your own lives and I respect that. But I want you to know that I want the best for you. I hope to see you soon and give you the biggest hug you've ever had! Your mother has done the best she could for you and Tom has been there for you also. Remember you always have a choice. My advice is to think about these choices and move forward in life. I want to thank you both for hanging in there and not giving up on me. I WILL NEVER GIVE UP ON YOU.

Thank you for being there when I needed you!

With love, I wish you a Merry Christmas too!
Dad

Christmas was tough that year. I spent it at Spectrum House giving out presents to the addicts just starting treatment. I could share my own experience with them, but more importantly, I was there to listen to their problems. Through my presence, I was able to offer them hope. There's simply no better way to stop worrying about your own troubles than by helping others. This was and still is a must for my recovery! After volunteering at Spectrum for a while, they offered me a job. I was honored and thrilled by this opportunity. I no longer had to work like a dog for minimal pay. Now I was able to do what I truly loved doing, helping other addicts. I began bringing some of the patients to AA meetings and up to that point I had not attended regularly myself.

The one thing I learned was that the first step in recovery consists of an admission of powerlessness. I applied it to my own life. Once I admitted defeat to drugs and alcohol, my recovery began! It was that simple. Admission of powerlessness equaled power over my addictions. One speaker at the meeting said that pride acts as a barrier to making any kind of admission. A lot of times an alcoholic would rather die than admit he has a problem. He also went on to say that alcohol and drug use is merely the symptom of a disease; it is the behavior that needs to be changed. BEHAVIORS! I could see it clearly that night. I needed to follow this program of action. There was a way up and a way out of this messy bog, and it was there for the taking. Someone later came up to me and handed me a blue book. At first I said I didn't need it, after all, I had a diploma! But just enough humility entered into my heart to accept that gift. Next to the Bible, it was to be the most important book I would ever read!

I started going to a meeting every week. I was told to ask God everyday to keep me from a drink or drug and thank Him at night if I stayed sober and this I did. I had this sense of urgency to help others and spread the word. I ran recovery groups at Spectrum and by now, was actually beginning to feel happier because helping others was, in turn, helping me even more so. I experienced peace and gratitude, making my life more manageable. As time went on, I had a stronger defense against the urge to pick up a drink or drug. I was told that the first time picking up would kill me, not the hundredth. I was learning how to live again. I prayed for my children, for Ann, for other addicts. I also learned that my problem centered in my mind; that the insanity of an addict is his constant belief, that one day he'll be able to use in safety; that somehow, somewhere he can beat the odds and use drugs without losing everything. That was my insanity. This was where God had to intervene. He had to show me how to play out the whole tape inside my head so I would realize what could happen to me if I started using again. If that occurred, the best thing I had going for me was to end up back at Spectrum House.

While on the job at Spectrum, the doctor in detox asked to speak to me because he was very concerned about me. "Don," he said. "Are you okay?" I answered, "Yes. Why?" "What's up with you, Don?" to which I replied, " I have no idea what you're implying." "Well, have you been getting high?" "No, what makes you ask?" "Do you have a wife by the name of Ann?" I answered yes, but that I had not lived with her for about three years. Then my next question was, "Is she active?" "You're damn right she is!" was his answer. He went on to tell me that he had just examined her at the clinic in downtown Worcester, and that she was strung out badly, looking terrible. He said he put her on the Methadone Program—long term.

No one ever knew what happened that day between the doc and myself, even though I knew in my heart something was not right all along by the questions he was asking me. This was just one way of God's truth being revealed to me. The news about Ann still hurt like a knife in my heart. I kept saying, "Turn it over" and "one day at a time". I prayed for Ann every day but realized that all the prayer in the world would not help another addict until he or she wanted to stay SOBER!

'How deep the empty bottomless Pit?
Saying goodbye is the hardest part of it.'

I went to God and prayed to be restored to sanity in all areas of my life. I prayed that my sick self-will be turned over to God. God's will was for me to stay sober and recover spiritually from this deadly illness. Everyday I turned my will and my life over to the care of God, as I understood Him. He was like a life-guard watching over me as I swam and as long as I didn't swim too far from Him, I would know He was there and would never let me drown. But, who was this God? The God I grew up with in the Episcopal Church was not working in my life. How could God have let all these things happen to me? This was no lifeguard! I had to start over with God. I needed a new relationship: Out with the old tapes and in with the new. But I didn't have to wait until I found out who God really was before I went to Him.

When I prayed for His will and not mine to be done, I simply had an easier time with life. I didn't question it then and I don't now. I had to make a decision and that was to have God run my life. He was going to be my new boss, my new employer, because He wants me to be happy and sane. He is compassionate and forgiving. My God lets me make mistakes so I can learn from them. God heals, healing me from all my wounds and transgressions. When I seek Him out, He is always ready to help me. To me the difference between religion and spirituality is simple; religion is for people who are afraid to go to Hell, while spirituality is for people who have already been to Hell and don't want to go back. That is why I needed an 'un-fearing' God in my life, someone who would love me the way I was at the moment, since I felt so defective. I abandoned myself to God as I understood Him and did not hold back... but...stepped out in faith!

I was three years sober when my friend Jesse died. I could count on one hand the number of close friends that I have had in my life...and Jesse was number one. The life I was leading left little room for trust, because addicts will lie right to your face if they think they can get something from or out of you. But Jesse and I trusted each other and knew that to have one true friend in a life of hell was much more important than ripping off one more addict. This is why it was hard for me to understand why an addict like me gets a second chance at this wonderful life while Jesse dies an addict's death!

Life's Perplexities

'What I am, I cannot change!
What I want, I cannot have!
What I need, I cannot get!
What I see, I cannot find!
What I know, I cannot grasp!'

And so...on a Sunday morning, Jesse's mother went to his bedroom to wake him up. She no doubt felt the dread that people feel when they see someone they love going down. This morning, her deepest fears came true. Jesse was dead at the young age of thirty-three.

'Life's so short that sometimes we're gone before we begin.'

I went to the funeral sober. I couldn't help thinking that I may have been able to do something to save him. Watching his shattered mother break down at the funeral hit my soul like a freight train. Hopefully, for his sake, Jesse is at peace with God.

Jesse's death hit me pretty hard emotionally. I had these feelings of rage and shame and guilt. It made me very angry and, of course, behind every angry emotion is FEAR. I asked myself what do I do now? Here I stood, three years without drugs, I had lost my best friend to an overdose and found myself still estranged from my family. I was at a loss as to what to do. There was one thing I knew I had to do and that was to ask someone for help, because if I realized that if I closed up I was a dead man. I had to take the shields off and break my isolation from my fellow man. I likened it to the old movies I used to watch, when the knights dressed in armor and prepared for battle. The armor for me was my defenses. I had so many years of dammed up emotions and fears buried underneath this armor. Jesse's death pierced that armor, for it was the first time in many, many years that I'd felt anything without drugs in my system! Someone once said to me that some addicts love you so much they will die for you in order to see you recover. I believe Jesse's death propelled me into a spiritual program of action, which would change every fiber of my being. I was about to be REBORN.

A Searching and Fearless Moral Inventory...

I needed to go back. I needed to face my past. I needed to search out those things in me that caused me to lack the ability to live life on life's terms. I was going to look back to understand why I was still suffering from the remorse and shame of yesterday. I was told to write a fearless and moral inventory of myself, to look at my BEHAVIORS. If I could see my patterns of destructive behavior, I could begin to live in the 'Solution' not the 'Problem'. All of it had to be dealt with; the inadequacies, the fears, the doubts and the sexual conduct. People are either acting on fear or faith, but now, I had to do it all on faith. We're all afraid to an extent to turn over our stones, but this was exactly what I had to do in order to survive.

'Many people Can't because they Won' t and few people Can because they Will!'

I always felt a little different than my fellow man. I didn't have enough money, power or prestige. I would say, look at me but don't look too close! I needed more. More sex, more recognition, MORE of MORE. Too much was never enough. My instincts ran riot (unchecked) and left me empty and afraid. Fear generated all sorts of absurd behavior. The bottom line was this: I felt inadequate and wanted to battle my way to the top, always seeking validation and approval from others. Again my pride was stopping me from writing this stuff out. I would have to write about my marriage, my family and my traumas. It was my inventory. I had to look at ME not anyone else. What have I done to hurt others and why? By this means I could begin to construct a moral sensibility; that is, to know RIGHT from WRONG. I had to stop running away from me. Faith is doing things without knowing the outcome. Mother Theresa said she was afraid every minute of her life but never let it stop her from doing anything she felt compelled to do!

I went to see Father Fred, a Roman Catholic priest, spending three hours with him. He too was in recovery and I heard that he had helped many alcoholics who were having trouble with their past. My hope was that he would tell me I was okay. Fred was going blind and couldn't see the coffee cup on the table. I had to move the cup where he was pouring the coffee. He opened that blue book that was given to me at my first AA meeting and pointed at it. It was a prayer that talked of making a decision to turn your will over to the care of God.

He wanted me to figure out on my own that I was already there and didn't even know it! It then dawned on me that I could write this inventory, because God was running the show and he would take care of me!

Chapter 9

Coming Out Of The Fog

'No one can promise a dream come true.
Stepping out in faith depends solely on you.'

After years of alcohol and drug abuse, denying my past and hurting myself, I had now been sober for three years. To continue on that narrow path required a willingness to examine my own behavior in terms of what flawed areas needed to be changed. This is called taking a personal inventory of your character defects. In other words, it's focusing on how and why you hurt other people, not on what those individuals did to hurt you.

In every situation I had become accustomed to being filled with fear, anger and self-pity, wanting to change the outside before I would the inside. I believed the only way to change was by acknowledging five things: Who I am. Where I am. Where I have come from. Where I want to go. And what am I doing to get in my own way getting there.

'Small strides are still Big
When they change the direction of a
Path off course!'

Despite my hellish past, I chose to both love and accept myself and get on my knees each morning and ask God to remove any fear I had about the day and to remove any desire for a drink or drug. Though I was sober, smoking one and a half packs of cigarettes was still part of my daily routine. To me, I still had another addiction to battle, another drug to overcome.

This was the re-birth of Donnie Steiger that included attending AA meetings regularly and striving not to hurt myself or anyone else again.

In trying to lead a normal life, I had ignored the pain of fear, hate, jealously and anger turned inward (depression) but now for the first time in my life, I came to understand my true motives of seeking to ease my pain, while continuing to hurt myself. You can refer to this as 'sabotaging' your life by living with fear and uncertainty and attempting to sooth the pain with drugs and alcohol. This kind of existence only makes your faults, weaknesses, failures and inadequacies STAND OUT more, which, in turn, prompts a continuous replay of all the unresolved issues. For me, it involved to name a few; fear of failing as a father and the shame of not knowing how to read and write. Coming to terms with my own 'defects' was not a pleasant experience nor for anyone who wants to improve him or herself, because our 'character flaws' can only hurt us, since denial only works until we can face the truth about ourselves. That's why our society is going at such a fast, reckless pace. Everyone is busy being in denial of his or her own pain, not stopping to take the time to deal with it in order to find healing!

'Although you see a new life that's free,
The change of new frightens me!'

I had two choices facing me: first, I could be willing to face the truth about myself or I could simply refuse to do so. But I discovered that in facing all my shortcomings there was security and spiritual growth in learning how to accept others and myself just as we are, which is still very difficult to practice. Part of my ability to stay sober every day was in taking inventory of the exact nature of my wrongs, because in the past, I felt it was me who had always been wronged and I could never believe that I owed anyone an apology. Believing this only leads a person to commit the continuous cycle of abuse against others and one's self.

There were plenty of escapes along the way. Relationships were one way of avoidance and escape. The best way to find out how you're going to act in a relationship is to get in one, period! Because, through it you'll learn exactly in what areas you are the weakest. I discovered that relationships are the 'miracle grow' to character defects. Until you find out what they are and deal with them, you'll never succeed in one. Whenever I felt that a relationship I was in was threatened or I experienced jealousy, I would always automatically detach by shutting down, closing up, locking the doors and building walls to isolate myself in solitude.

One way that helped me stay in touch with the realities of my shortcomings was by playing in a sober rock band. I found it to be encouraging, hanging around people trying to stay sober like me, because in a band, egos can get in the way and start the fire of dissension among its members. We had to learn that even though each of us was different, in order to be successful performers...we had to act as one 'undivided unit' (although I still managed to get my three minute drum solos in!)

But the last thing I wanted to do was give up those character defects, which had always worked so well for me. But I did...I had to if I wanted to get better. I looked at my sexual conduct, fear, insecurity, jealousy and anger and realized that rather then acknowledge them, I acted out in rage to hurt others and myself as well. Yes, even in sobriety.

One of the main problems in being detached from everything and everyone is that it starts to make you very sick. This happened to me when I was too embarrassed to share with anyone my illiteracy, usually, because someone, sooner or later, would tell me to get my GED or do this or that. I got very tired of hearing that since what is easy for one person may not be so easy for another. I have come to learn something very important about myself: I have been blessed with common sense and practical wisdom, whereas someone considered to be intelligent my not possess those qualities. One reason why I had kept people at bay was because I had always felt that I was retarded, not a good person, not worthy of anything good in my imperfect world. And so, to hide my true feelings from others, I put on a facade that everything was okay. Which worked...until I got sober. Then I couldn't stuff it any longer. I had to have a new attitude if I were going to overcome my denial. I had to step-out in faith, making it a daily challenge to stay sober and at peace with myself. Sadly, many people never overcome their denial. I consider myself to have made significant strides in dealing with my own denial.

ACCEPTING RESPONSIBILITY FIRST CORRECTING IRRESPONSIBILITY SECOND

All of this took time and effort to remain committed to that goal. Working three jobs, I had very little money (paying child support, going through a divorce) to spend beyond the basics necessary for living. It is very hard to accept life on life's terms when you've spent most of your life masking all the pain so that others can't see it. I had to come to the realization that it was me who made my mistakes and had created my own mess and therefore it was me who must set about the task of correcting them! Telling another person the exact nature of all my wrongs was the first step of being honest with God, another human being and myself.

Divorce

'Bringing forth man's duty
To provide and protect...
An expectation of unforgiving society
...I had to neglect .'

The relationships that were to come in sobriety after my divorce with women in particular would be co-dependent in nature. To stay sober, I couldn't remain with someone who continued to use. If it were not a matter of life and death, I would never have left Ann. I still loved her then and I still care about her well being today. I am truly sorry for the failing of our marriage and pray for her forgiveness. I made a sincere commitment to stay clean and sober, whatever it took. This was one of the few times in my life that I decided to take a positive stand. Yet, I found that going to AA meetings regularly had become, at this stage, frustrating because my ex was not allowing me to see my own children. Sometimes I would attend a meeting and just scream at the top of my lungs when it came time to introduce myself, after holding everything in until I got there. This freaked out a lot of people and you know, it worked! Because what better place to do it! Many members came over to me afterwards and would say 'its going to be all right'. And I knew it would be, but it was going to be a very frustrating journey that lay ahead of me. Verbally venting out loud was not only expressing my frustration but for time it was also a way of telling myself: I am not a victim anymore. I don't need to be full of self-pity. I no longer have to pull others into my mess. I am now being responsible.

Another Charlie's Surplus road race, 1993.

Chapter 10

Mother

Searching for Answers
"Why have you gone, where did you go?
I'll never be the same, how will I grow?
Help me, mom, I can't find my way!
I need you with me to guide me each day."

After being in a relationship for two years, my insecurities again surfaced and Christine and I split up. This was devastating to me because I was very much in love with her and we had become quite attached to one another. As a result, I became deeply depressed and down on life in general, this after being sober for five years. I had lost my job, car and apartment, therefore broke, making it necessary to live with my father—a big let down after struggling for so long to afford a place of my own.

There were days when I found myself sitting on the end of my bed and staring across the room crying, not fully understanding why. Since I didn't know then why this was happening to me, I took another inventory and noticed that the people on my list didn't include the name of my mother. I couldn't grasp why I was able to forgive and ask to be forgiven by them but not do the same for my own mother. The one thing I did feel was that my Mom really didn't matter. I asked myself, "What did I ever do to her, anyway?" This is the woman who beat and abandoned me! So at the wise suggestion of a friend to do a thorough accounting of my actions, I wrote her name down on my list and asked, "How have I wronged her?" And I came up with these three wrongs:

1. I hated her.
2. I resented her.
3. I was angry with her.

Now I understood why her name had been missing from the list since the start of my sobriety.

While writing these reasons, I began crying because I knew in my heart that for the first time in the denial of my mother the truth had revealed itself: she was an alcoholic. She might have had it worse than me (taking all the pain and unhappiness out on my father, my brother, my sister, myself and herself).

Releasing all these pent-up emotions I carried my entire life, I decided I needed to call her after no contact for 28 years, in order to make my amends. I did this, not knowing where she lived, not knowing if I would ever see her again. Within 24 hours of praying for the chance to make things right with my mother, my brother Eddie (not aware of my prayer) came to the door and asked if I wanted our mother's phone number. When I said yes, I turned to him and asked, "Guess what! Do you know that Mom's an alcoholic?" He replied, "Yeah, Don. I know." "But Eddie," I said. "She's an alcoholic who might have had it far worse then we ever did." All he could say was, "Yeah, yeah, yeah. I'll see ya later!" Giving me the number, he turned and walked away.

I called Sue and went over to her place to use the phone. My Mom answered the phone and said, "Hello." and I said the word "MOM." Then she said, "Donnie." These same two words, not uttered in 28 years were repeated several times before the conversation continued. After this we both began crying uncontrollably and I had to turn the phone over to Sue, not able to continue speaking. This moment was an intense healing experience for me! I was determined to talk to her whether she was in a nursing home or living alone, whether sober or not. Just to tell her, "Mom, I AM SORRY."

So my sister and I made arrangements to visit Mom in Philadelphia. When we arrived at her place and got off the elevator, the first thing she did was take me inside her apartment, sit me down on the couch, grab both my hands, look straight into my eyes and with tears running down her cheeks, she told me how sorry she was and how much she had missed me, and now realized how much she had hurt, not only me, but all of us. That moment is something I shall never forget! This was my mom making amends to me and it took me by surprise. After all, I had come with the intention of expressing my need for her forgiveness. At that time, Mom had been sober for ten years. I learned that she had been in several detox programs and halfway houses but, most importantly, she too could not read or write. Now I knew why she would always yell at me all the time; being frustrated with her own illiteracy and too embarrassed to admit it to her kids.

I decided that I was going to move my mother back to Worcester in order to establish a relationship with her for the first time in my life at the age of forty-six. I tried to spend all my spare time at her home, especially on the holidays! We would attend meetings together occasionally. During this 'healing process' I began to find out more about the woman I was now proud to call my mother. I learned about her past history, that she was brought up poor in the backwoods of Tennessee without any formal education. At a very early age she had been pulled out of school to take care of her dying father.

We were able to develop a very loving and compassionate bond and I could, for the first time ever, have the love I had for her without holding the past against her. There was no way that I would allow the past to RUIN the present! Not after being given the unexpected gift of having a 'Mom' in my life again for a brand new start. I heard this saying while watching the movie "Magnolia" which portrayed the 'healing prophecies' of its characters:

'Sometimes we may be through with our past
but...
Our past may not be through with us.'

Our world is full of people who can't handle the present because they are still holding on to the resentments of the past.

My mom and I started attending a Pentecostal church together because I had come to know the pastor, Joey, as a personal friend. He would preach, play rhythm guitar and sing in the praise and worship hour. I also began playing my drums. It was something I enjoyed doing as a way of giving back to God for what he had done for me—REMOVING THE DESIRE TO DRINK AND DRUG!

'Set me free. Set me free. Set me free.
I am free. I am free. I am free.
Thank you. Thank you. Thank you.'

There were moments when my mom and I would just stand at the alter, holding hands while praying, the tears flowing down our faces...evidence that the barriers between us were breaking down and bringing further healing to people who were once alienated in body, mind and spirit.

Soon after we were baptized together, my mom noticed pain in her legs. An examination revealed that she had breast cancer. They removed one breast and part of her lung. She underwent chemotherapy for one year. Needless to say, this was a very difficult time for us both. But I loved her and wanted to be with her, especially now. Having this opportunity was something I considered a gift in itself. Now she could have someone with her, not needing to endure it alone.

She did, in time, get better, only to fall ill again about a year later. She received the bad news that the cancer had spread to her liver and the diagnosis was that she only had three months to live. This was hard news to accept, because my mother and I had just begun to know and love one another the way it should be in a normal family. I could have reacted to this situation in a negative way and shut off everything and everyone around me, blaming God for breaking up what had just been put back together again. But I said, "Okay, Mom. What is it you want me to do?" Her answer: "I want to stay in my own apartment to die, not go to a nursing home." When I asked her again, her response matched the first answer. "That's all." She then asked if I would be with her through it all, saying in the same breath, "You've got other things to do, I'm not all that important." But I assured her, "Yes Mom, you are important! To me you are the most important person in my life!"

I contacted Hospice so that they could help me bathe her and show me how to administer drugs to her whenever they weren't there such as morphine patches, demoral and tranquilizers. The Hospice people considered me to be a 'caretaker' for my mother and I am indebted to them for their assistance.

We watched her favorite television programs and talked about different things that would help, in some way, keep her mind off the pain. Often times, I would kneel by her bed, hold her hand and pray with her. I would also continuously read the bible and kept remembering day and night, the verse "This too shall pass." The kind of pain I was experiencing did not afflict my body but only the heart—a loving pain that comes from caring for someone close whom you love unconditionally no matter what!

'Forever is one day at a time.
One day sometimes seems like Forever...'

Never in my life did I, nor could I imagine that in getting sober and coming to a personal relationship with my 'Higher power' whom I chose to call God, that I would be giving the drug of my choice to someone I had come to love and care about so deeply! I had asked God daily to remove the obsession for a drug or a drink and here I was...having all these drugs right in front of my eyes and not once get the urge to pick up and start using them again! That, to me was remarkable, a miracle in itself, besides which, having the capacity to care for my mother after having undergone a case of severe depression. It was the healing process between us that helped me to be there for her whether she was well or sick. What better gift?

For you the reader, there are several points I wish to make:

Whatever has been done to you by your mother or father
remember they have brought you into this world
and did their best to raise you. Forgiveness is not so
much for them as it is for you. One can't sit around
waiting for someone to ask for his or her forgiveness,
because that day may never come. A person must take the
first step himself before it is too late!
We must forgive ourselves first for carrying anger
and resentments held against a parent. To verbally
forgive them is allowing yourself to hear the words...
"I forgive you."
It's saying I do, in fact, without hesitation or reservation
FORGIVE.

The act of saying and hearing...I forgive you can be summarized into three parts: First, forgiveness involves making a decision. It is to realize that carrying around resentments has made you sick. Second, forgiveness involves recognizing what it is that you need to forgive and then verbally telling the person the reason why you are forgiving and to genuinely mean it. For unless it's done in sincerity, it will all be for nothing! Third, forgiveness involves a continuing process. It is persevering along the steady Forgiveness Road, aware that it is an act, a decision to practice daily in all your relations with family, friends and co-workers.

Finally, when my mother did pass away, in only two months rather than three, it was a most unusual experience for me, because I had never before seen anyone die in my presence. I called the hospice nurse and asked her to come over as she asked me to do, in order to help me flush all the drugs down the toilet. There was no one there for me to answer to, but all alone, I had come to terms with the fact not to use drugs. For me to use following my mother's death in her place is something I don't believe I could have ever recovered from. The nurse already knew that I was a recovering addict because I wanted to tell on my disease which is great inventory, especially if you're going to be trusted to administer them.

Throughout this ordeal, I was never in tears, but was able to make the necessary arrangements required at someone's passing. It felt like my mom was still there with me and now, instead of all the years of abuse preceding this event, I kept seeing my mother giving me reassurance, love and security, things I had never received before our reconciliation. Doing so had opened up a spiritual avenue for growth in myself as well as being there for Mom on 'good terms', with mended hearts to say good-bye. Up until that point, my mother was only in my heart in the form of anger. My thoughts of her were only of hatred. I could never identify with anyone as a mother figure, which I'm sure had a lot to do with my poor relationships with other women.

The most important thing I got from this whole experience of renewal with my mother is the happy memories of ultimately being together to share our love and lives. The void in my heart had now been filled and even with her passing, I am grateful to have had the gift of getting to know her, love her, and accept her...as my mother! My spirit is, and will always be, enriched with the wonderful feelings of someone who, by God's grace, turned out to be the wonderful mother for whom I had always been looking. Today my relationships with women have improved and, most importantly, I now have different tapes of my mother to play and replay until I see her again!

Never Too Late
'It's NEVER too LATE to be a father.
It's NEVER too LATE to be a Mother.
It's NEVER too LATE to be a Son.

It's NEVER too LATE to be a Daughter.
It's NEVER too LATE to be a Brother.
It's NEVER too LATE to be a Sister.
It's NEVER too LATE to be a Friend.
Until the END, then it's too LATE.'
(Unless you want to make amends to a slab of marble.)

Reunited with our mother (left to right): Sue, myself, Mom, Ed, early 1980's.

Chapter 11

Boston Marathon (Back of the Pack) 2000

Running
'When I'm running, the wind whistles through my ears
Sweat instead of fears.
One more mile, there goes another trial,
A pretty girl at which I smile.
Pick up the pace, for in running on time,
Got to keep in shape, no time to wait.
A car pulls out in front of me...
I stop and look—you almost hit me!
Get going again, there is sweat on my chin,
I looked around the many sights that are free.
The world that God made just for me!
Thank you for my health, for you see...
I am so lucky to have me.
The greatest gift of all, Life.'

With the draining and time consuming days of caring for my mother behind me, it was now time to increase my training for the approaching Boston Marathon. This would be my first time running it, at the age of 50. My last one was 22 years ago in the 'Silver Lake Dodge Marathon' when I was 28 years old. Up to this point, I had put in 25-30 miles of running each week and thought why not run Boston, after training for almost six months. So I picked up the pace and began adding more miles little by little, conditioning my body to go the distance (26.2 miles). I also included swimming and weight lifting as part of my daily work out, which doesn't hurt! So after completing one 18 and 19 milers respectively and two 20 milers, I was ready! I soon purchased my bus ticket that would take me to Hopkington, Massachusetts where the race begins. I was positioned in the back, way back with the other 'bandits' in the field. As I looked around, all I could see were thousands upon thousands of other runners, more than 17,000, the most ever in the race's history.

After the gun went off I was several miles into the run, something happened to my awareness that would tell the real story of the Boston Marathon. Something more than just the top elite runners competing to win and have the wreath of victory placed on their head. For in looking over to my left I observed an overweight woman with a huge written letter on her back that read: Angela Sommers (fictitious name) died August 19,1999 of breast cancer. The letter expressed how much she loved her mother. The woman was running to raise money for cancer research. To my right, I saw a man whose leg had been amputated, walking on crutches. And man, he was really kickin' it in too! In front of me was a young man in his 20's sitting in a wheelchair with 'cerebral palsy'. His body was so twisted that his head was looking over his left shoulder while scooting himself along going backwards! Each of these people having, heart and determination, were going their own pace, inch by painstaking inch just to finish no matter what the cost physically and mentally!

As I passed them, many more stories came into focus. I noticed the thousands of spectators lining the route that were clapping and whistling and listening to the bands play. Young and old alike were handing out oranges, water, vaseline, wet-naps and sports drinks. That's when I was able to identify with everyone and have my faith in humanity restored just a little more! I reflected upon all that I had gone through in order to get to this point in my life, and being healthy and fit enough to run in this historical new millennium marathon and finish with a time of 4:30. Above the noise of the crowd, I could hear my mother calling my name, "Donnie! Donnie!" I had a deep sense of her presence with me as a means of support. Though my journey had not been identical to that of most people, I was able to grasp the truth that sometimes in life we're waiting, sometimes we're listening and sometimes there are down hills and up hills to face! Never forgetting that when cresting the top, there is always a cool breeze and the wind whistling as you look to the flats below. Understand that there will always be the hills (trials) and the flats (easy times) and the valleys (down times), which are the challenge of enduring the testing of your personal goals and ambitions!

Allow yourself to accept the hard fact that with any great task, if you want to get to the top of the hill (sometimes 'heartbreak' hill) and make it to the finish line...you are going to have to SUCK UP THE PURPLE BUTTERMILK!!!

Chapter 12

Going Home

'Home is where you know where you're at.
Home is where you hang your own hat.
Home is where you lay your own head.
Home is where you make your own bed.'

I have come to believe that when the decision was made to go home, I was actually seeking peace...peace of mind and peace of spirit. I was full of fear, that the feelings would overwhelm me, but it wasn't like that at all. It was gratitude, forgiveness and sadness for the little boy who did not have a chance in 1950. To be standing right there, knowing how hard I had worked to return here, letting out all the welled-up tears, after so many, many years of painful memories and joyous accomplishments, was something I never dreamed could ever happen!

While looking at the house in which I have cherished the most, and that is the only place I'll always consider to be my real home, I kept saying to myself, "I'm okay. I'm okay." "I made it! I made it!" "Remembering and letting go!" "Remembering and letting go!" "I'm home! I'm home!" "I love you, Donnie!" "I love myself and I will do whatever it takes to survive!"

I did not want to leave Hawthorne, the home of my childhood that day, but in reality, I did not want to leave myself anymore or escape for I felt that I was home now and that is where I'll stay.

Welcome Home, Donnie! Welcome Home!

Straight Shooter in Haight Ashbury: me posing with a homeless man in San Francisco during my summer 2000 trip to California.

Appendix

November 15, 1998

Dear Old Good Old Donnie,

I hope you are enjoying all the blessings of life when you read this letter. I am doing just great!

Thank you for the photograph you sent me. I treasure it ever much! Looking at it brought a lot of memories to me. I guess things and feelings I shared those three months I spent at Spectrum House with all you guys made a great impression on me. I'll never forget! It's like a special bond that holds us together, having gone through a dramatic stage of our lives. A significant love, like no other, grows to the point that we become true family.

I remember the very first night I spent at 'The House'. You came and took the time to talk to me about how things were supposed to be done, while at the same time you were helping me to do my bed. Right then, I knew you were a loving father and I could see right away your good nature. I'll never forget the way you helped me, like that night that they gave me 'spare parts', when I couldn't stop crying even after we all went to bed. You were the only one who came over to my bedside to hug and comfort me just like a big brother. I have blessed you ever since, Donnie, and by God's grace I always do! Don't you ever forget that you are a good man, a great friend and should feel proud about your good-natured gift endowed by God Himself! Those who would not see this are just plain ignorant and we bless them too! So don't take shit from no one. Be patient. There will be someone who will notice this high-priced quality in you and value you for what you are. But better yet, be good to your own self!

Well, Pal, as I told you over the phone, I am taking care of my family's business, managing our properties. I have a daughter ten and a four-year old boy. I go to 'Narcotics Anonymous' and for the last eleven years, I feel great!

I might come over to see all of you guys next summer or next September. I'll surely let you know.

Well, Buddy, take care of yourself and we'll talk real soon!

Love,

Raul Velazquez

Miscellaneous Pictures of Interest

Steve Connolly
Spirit of the KING®

One of the top Elvis impersonators in Las Vegas, Stephen Connolly.

Amy's graduation picture, 1995.

My father and Clayton Moore (The Lone Ranger) in Las Vegas, 1996.

Jesse (21 years old) drivin' on highway A1A in Fort Lauderdale, 1997.

Life isn't over...just because you're sober! Livin' it up in Fort Lauderdale, 1997.

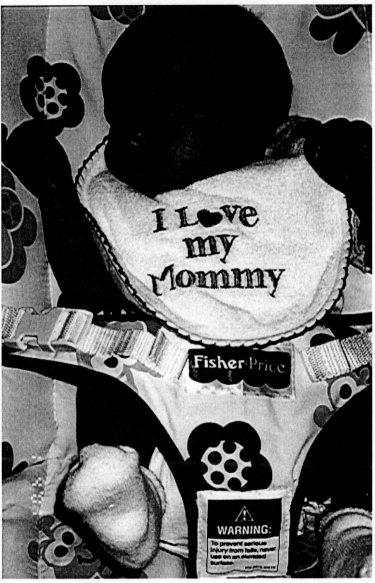

Another reason to stay sober: my first grandchild, John Otis Steiger, born December 29, 2000 to parents Jesse and Stephanie.

Vacationing in Fort Lauderdale, January, 2001.

Pun & Poem Index

—by Don Steiger

—by John Lynch

—by Jim Puz

Books Recommended by the Author

The Bible

Carlson, Richard, *Don't Sweat the Small Stuff*, Hyperion Books, New York, 1997

Chandler, Steve, *100 Ways To Motivate Yourself*, Career Press, Franklin Lakes, New Jersey, 1996, To order call 1-800-CAREER-1

Engstrom, Ted, *The Pursuit of Excellence*, Zondervan Publishing House, Grand Rapids, MI, 1982

Father Fred and the Twelve Steps, Ambassador Books, Worcester, MA, 1996, To order call 1-800-577-0909

Johnson, Michael (Olympic Gold Medallist), *Slaying the Dragon*, Regan Books, New York, 1996, For information please write: Special Markets Department,   Harper Collins Publishers, Inc., 10 East 53rd Street, New York, NY 10022

Lindquist, Marie, *Holding Back (why we hide the truth about ourselves)*, Hazelden Foundation, Center City, MN, 1987, for order information, call 1-800-328-9000

Richardson, Jennifer, *diary of ABUSE/diary of HEALING, Recovery Communications*, Baltimore, 1996, For information, call 1-410-243-8558

Silverstein, Shel, *The Giving Tree*, Harper Collins Publishers, New York, 1964

Williams, Margery, *The Velveteen Rabbit or How Toys Became Real*, Running Press, Philadelphia, 1998, To order check your local bookstore or write to: Running Press Book Publishers, 125 South 22nd Street, Philadelphia, PA 19103-4399

Secret of Life

'Take time to THINK. It is the source of POWER.
Take time to PLAY. It is the secret of perpetual YOUTH.
Take time to be FRIENDLY. It is the road the HAPPINESS.
Take time to WORK. It is the price of SUCCESS.
Take time to PRAY. It is the greatest power on EARTH.
Take time to LOVE and be LOVED.
It is the way of GOD.'
— copied, author unknown

God Bless America

In memory of those who lost their lives and their loved ones on
September 11, 2001

Ordering Information

To order books, please call   1-508-892-4683

Fax: 1-508-892-3814

Or E-mail: Purplebuttermilk@charter.net

To order by mail, write to: Tabitha Connolly
P.O. Box 337
Leicester, MA 01524

Cost per book: $12.00

*Note: Checks or money orders only in US Funds made out to Purple Buttermilk.

ABOUT THE AUTHOR

My name is Don and I am a part Cherokee Indian who was born in southern California, but now live in Worcester, Massachusetts.

ABOUT GREATUNPUBLISHED.COM

www.greatunpublished.com is a website that exists to serve writers and readers, and to remove some of the commercial barriers between them. When you purchase a GreatUNpublished title, whether you order it in electronic form or in a paperback volume, the author is receiving a majority of the post-production revenue.

A GreatUNpublished book is never out of stock, and always available, because each book is printed on-demand, as it is ordered.

A portion of the site's share of profits is channeled into literacy programs.

So by purchasing this title from GreatUNpublished, you are helping to revolutionize the publishing industry for the benefit of writers and readers.

And for this we thank you.